The Cat Flap

By Dennis Diamond and Patrick Blosse

A play in three acts for lovers of Agatha Christie

5 female / 5 male

DiaBlo Publishing

Published by DiaBlo Publishing, 2024

ISBN: 9798320881164

First edition

Printed by Kindle Direct Publishing in the United Kingdom

Other books by Pat Blosse:

Novels and Short Stories

The Red Bonnet (a supernatural mystery thriller)

Short and Sweet: 100-Word Stories

Plays

Heaven's Above (one-act play for children)

There Will be Some Slight Interference (one-act play)

In collaboration with Dennis Diamond

   The Ghosts of Martha Rudd (three-act ghostly comedy)

   Lost But Not Least (one-act Shakespearean drama)

   Sketches in Hyde Park (5-part radio play)

Contact:

patblosse@gmail.com or

on Facebook at Patrick Blosse_Author Page

Copyright © 2024: Dennis S Diamond and Patrick G Blosse

All Rights Reserved

The characters and events portrayed in this play are fictitious. Any similarity to real persons, living or dead, is coincidental and not intended by the authors.

No part of this book may be reproduced, or stored in a retrieval system, or transmitted in any form or by any means, electronic, mechanical, photocopying, recording, or otherwise, without express written permission of the publisher.

Licencing

Enquiries about licencing for amateur and professional performances and readings should be sent to patblosse@gmail.com.

References to background music and other stage effects are for guidance only. Please replace these with music, effects etc. that are suitable for your own production and for which you have obtained appropriate licences.

Contents

		Page
Synopsis		5
Cast of Characters		8
The Setting		12
Act One	November 1963. Evening. The kitchen of a Devon longhouse	16
Act Two	Christmas Eve, 1963. Evening	61
Act Three, Scene One	July 1964 Afternoon	101
Act Three, Scene Two	Morning of the next day	139
Properties List		176
Sound Effects		182
Lighting Effects		191
Visual Effects		196

Synopsis

The Cat Flap is a comedy-thriller in three acts with a cast of 10 (5 male, 5 female). Characters' ages range from late teens to about 80. One actor inhabits 5 personalities. The action takes place between November 1963 and July 1964.

The play is an unapologetic celebration of Agatha Christie's body of work. All the usual elements are here: unexplained deaths, a large handful of potential suspects, red herrings, an amateur detective, a bumbling bobby, and a bristling colonel with a loaded 12-bore. What's more, it's packed to the gunwales with anagrams and affectionate references to Christie titles, characters and plots (and some that are dropped in with the subtlety of a house-brick). If you don't like the play, you can spend a couple of hours happily searching them out. But this is not meant to be an intellectual exercise. This is a play for when you fancy a good night out and a bit of a laugh.

Mavis Hadley lives in a historic longhouse in the West Country where she runs a cattery. Old, run-down, and in need of a thorough make-over, but nonetheless, good with the cats, she lives with her younger brother, Scratchy, and his 17-year-old daughter, Louisa (Lulu). The house is owned by 'the Colonel'. She has lived there rent-free for 40 years (for reasons that will become apparent) but suddenly the Colonel has decided he wants it back. He appears to have a clandestine understanding with Scratchy that involves the building's cellar, which might or might not have something to do with the faulty boiler down there.

The Colonel's son, Tarquin (40) turns up unexpectedly, showing off his latest conquest, the actress Veronica Pigeon, who also has in tow her son, Walter. They too show an uncommon interest in the cellar. Thrown into the mix in act one are Mavis's next-door neighbour, Jean Palmer, whose many accomplishments include amateur sleuthing, an inept WPC with an unhealthy interest in Lulu, and finally a mysterious stranger in the shape of an ageing, ham, Shakespearian actor. It is probably a relief to discover that Mavis dies at the end of the act one while all but one of the cast are down in the cellar.

Act two moves the story on from the night that Kennedy died to Christmas Eve 1963. A blizzard and two unhelpful boilers conspire to lock the family and friends in the cattery. Walter and Lulu enjoy each other's company, but that cannot be said for anyone else. As tensions rise, another mysterious stranger arrives, a German plumber, causing the Colonel apoplexy. Luckily, he dies, which solves that problem.

It is 6 months later and the height of summer when we next catch up with the story. With both Mavis and the Colonel dead, Tarquin has inherited the house and Veronica (now Mrs Tarquin) has swept through the house like a new broom. That is to say, she supervised the sweeping. The long-suffering Scratchy has done all the work. The cattery has been closed down and Veronica unveils her plans for a 'Pussy Parlour'. So far, the "accidental deaths" have not attracted any police attention. In any case, WPC Hastings is far too concerned by the relationship between Walter and Lulu to take an interest in anything remotely like detective work.

That is Jean Palmer's prerogative. Yet another mysterious stranger arrives, the doddery Lady Hattie Chrisaga. But she is quickly unveiled as Veronica's (dead?) second husband, and when Jean's prime suspect, Tarquin, also dies mysteriously, it is time to call in Scotland Yard.

How this mess ever gets resolved and how New York's 34th Precinct D I Peter Colhouri get involved are explained in Act 3, Scene 2. Read it. It's fun.

Cast of Characters (5 F / 5 M)

MAVIS HADLEY (F) 60's. Unhappy woman, dishevelled, morose. Sister to Jack (Scratchy), aunt to Jack's daughter, Louisa 'Lulu' Hadley. Mavis' past is unclear, perhaps a romantic involvement many years earlier with Lt. Col. Bulstrode Pyke. She operates a cattery from her home in the West Country, where she lives with Scratchy and Lulu. A fairly short and dumpy woman with mousy hair that is rarely brushed. She is never seen without her worn, faded and stained housecoat and usually wears fingerless mittens whilst working in the cattery. Vague, absent-minded and invariably at odds with the people and things around her.

JACK 'SCRATCHY' HADLEY (M) 50's. Mavis' brother. They live together in a constant state of niggling antagonism. Lazy and unkempt, he avoids work as much as possible. He has a wooden leg, having lost one in the war, which cats use as a scratch post, hence his nickname. He spent the entire war in the Army Pay Corps barracks in Tiverton and lost his leg in motorbike accident whilst coming home on leave in 1944. He dotes on his daughter Lulu. Ex batman to Lt. Col. Bulstrode Pyke.

LOUISA 'Lulu' HADLEY (F) Older teenager. Scratchy's daughter. A modern, liberated girl still in the rebellious stage. Quite pretty. She has no memory of her mother who she was told had died giving birth to her. She is studying design at art college, makes most of her own clothes and is not afraid to experiment. She has ambitions to open a boutique in Carnaby Street although she has never ventured further east than Axminster. Bright and breezy character facing the modern age with relish. Despises her aunt Mavis, frowns on her father, Jack, but is protective of him. Has a series of boyfriends of dubious character, none of which we ever see, though we hear their motorbikes.

VERONICA PIGEON (F) 40's. Glamorous woman, married 3 times, widowed 3 times. An actress who was never a star but believes that she was. She tries to project an air of sophistication and breeding but the occasional slip in her speech or manners give away a more chequered past. Comes to the village at the invitation of her lover Tarquin Bulstrode Pyke. Did she perhaps once have a one-night stand with Tarquin's father, the Colonel, 20 years ago?

WALTER PIGEON (M) about 20. Gauche son of Veronica and smitten with Lulu at first meeting; tells her he would 'kill for her'. Good looking, studious and introverted. Unworldly and especially shy of women, he is desperate for a quiet, conventional life but his mother is equally keen for him to be the next screen heartthrob, frequently drags him off to auditions and contrives 'introductions' to people in the film industry. Walter is secretly studying accountancy by correspondence course, as he finds the subject "endlessly fascinating". Introduced to Lt. Col. Bulstrode Pyke early in the play, he is quickly hired as the Colonel's secretary. Could he possibly be the progeny of the Colonel and Veronica's one-night stand?

LT. COL. ALISTAIR BULSTRODE PYKE (M) 80's. Blustering old local landowner and chairman of the parish council, living at Maydmaster Manor with son Tarquin. Ex-Army, bigoted, racist, misogynistic, he is rarely seen without his loaded shotgun. Bristling moustache with bristling personality to match. He owns Mavis' cottage and is keen to terminate the lease for reasons that are at first unexplained. Served in India. Has a tic. He takes no prisoners.

TARQUIN BULSTRODE PYKE (M) Late 40's. Clarke Gable look-a-like, bit of a cad, not very bright. Manipulative and cruel but gullible when it comes to the ladies. He thinks he is the apple of Veronica's eye, but is she just using him to improve her prospects?

JEAN PALMER (F) 55-65. Mavis's next-door neighbour and only friend. A mad cat-lady and amateur sleuth. She models herself on Margaret Rutherford's version of Miss Marple, always wears tweeds and pearls and sports a tweed hat with a wide hatband with a long feather in it. She is constantly looking for mysteries to solve where none exist and is overjoyed by the death of President Kennedy because it gives her another case to solve. Most of her solutions are wide of the mark. Intelligent, interfering and excitable

WPC. HASTINGS (F) 30's. Lazy, unambitious, and slow-witted local Bobby. Dotes on Lulu and goes to questionably extreme lengths to protect her. Subject to fits of jealousy. Although written as a female character, this part could equally well be played as a male with minor adaptations to the script. Permission for such changes can be assumed.

THE MYSTERIOUS STRANGER Age about 40-50 but usually unclear due to heavy disguises used throughout; even 'his' gender might be uncertain. An ex-actor, he is the 2nd of Veronica's 3 'dead' husbands but appears in the guises of:

> **ARCHIE GATHASIT** [*gather-sit*] 70ish. an over-the-top ham actor with a resonating voice and an endless line in Shakespearian quotes. His disguise of white wig, cape and cane make him look like the original TV Dr Who.
>
> **ERICH THAAARGIST** [*Eric Thaagh-gist* (as in give not gist)] middle-aged. German plumber in 'traditional' German costume of feathered hat, braces, and lederhosen. Short tempered and irascible.
>
> **LADY HATTIE CHRISAGA** [*kris-aga* (as in the kitchen stove)] 60s. Something of a dowager duchess with wide brimmed hat, unflattering, ankle-length dress, and lorgnettes which she can both hide behind and use to poke at people.
>
> **DETECTIVE INSPECTOR PETER COLHOURI**, New York City Police (34th Precinct) [*coll-heuri*] 40s. This might be 1964 but he is dressed more like Philip Marlow from the 1940s. Felt hat, mackintosh, carries a cigar which he never lights. Quite a bad American accent which he can't maintain.

During the play we also hear the voices of various radio announcers and personalities, including **Leonard Parkin, Dan Maskell, Percy Thrower** and **Alvar Lidell**.

The Setting

The play is set in the kitchen/dining room of a semi-detached property in the West Country; a longhouse that was converted into farmer's cottages many years previously. The cottage has a boarding cattery in its back garden, apparently the principal means of income for the family. It sits within the grounds of Maydmaster Manor (pronounced Maid-master), the 'country seat' of Lt. Col. Bulstrode Pyke. The action starts on the evening of the announcement of President Kennedy's death in November 1963 and continues on Christmas Eve 1963 and the summer of 1964.

A large mirror hangs on the R of the back wall over a radio/telephone table with a cord-operated wall light above it. To the left of the table, in the centre of the back wall, are French doors that open out on to a small courtyard. Across the courtyard can be seen part of a series of run-down cattery pens. A peeling, hand-painted sign that says 'CatRy' is hanging at an angle from the corner of the nearest pen. A small 'B & B' signs hangs from the Catry sign by one string. An ancient outside light, festooned with spider webs, hangs at a slightly erratic angle above the outside of the French doors. The rest of the back wall is given over to a kitchen worktop with a Butler sink immediately to the left of the French doors, set at 90 degrees to the back wall, with a window over it that overlooks the cattery pens and a path leading from the French doors to the Jean Palmer's house next door. Lightweight gingham or floral-patterned curtains hide the area beneath the worktop. A small oven and hob stands in the UL corner and a large kitchen dresser displaying plates, cups, and saucers etc.is UL. The kitchen area is on a slightly raised dais. A door DL leads to the hallway, front door, and other rooms downstairs. UR, to the right of the radio/telephone table, is an archway with steps leading to the upstairs bedrooms. There is a row of coat hooks on the hidden wall inside the arch at the bottom of the stairs. A narrow door DR leads to the cellar. DS centre stands a large wooden kitchen table with 3 chairs. A big, old-fashioned radiogram stands on a table UR, to the left of the arch, next to a 1950s style black telephone.

It is the evening of 22nd November 1963. A large wall clock on the wall above the radio/telephone table shows 6:58.

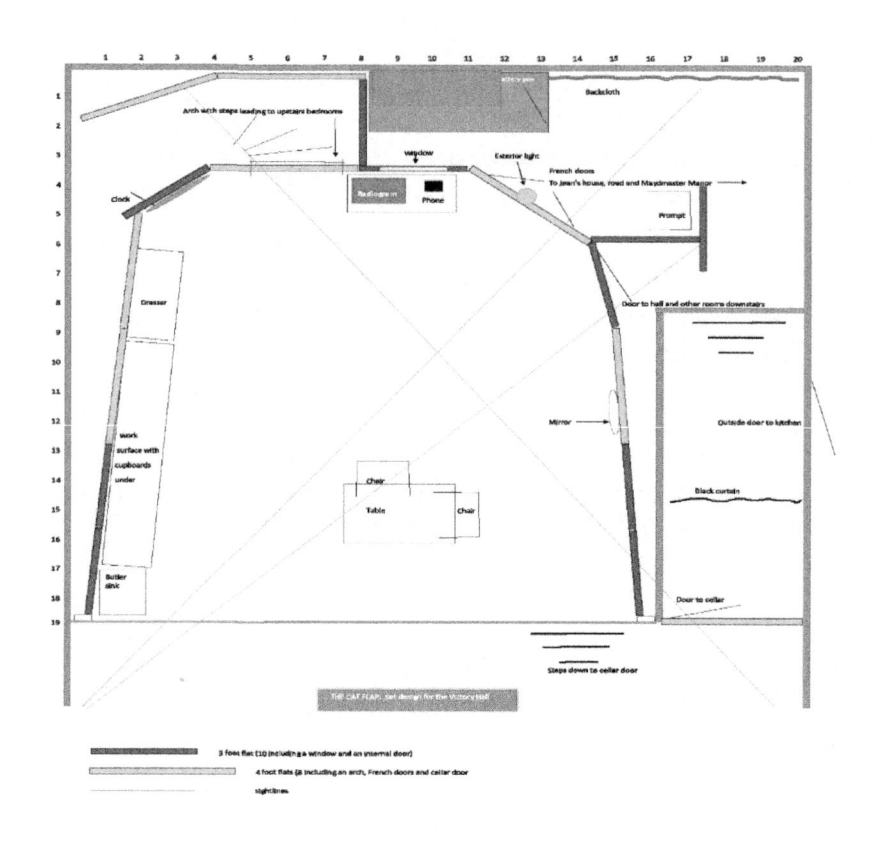

This set was designed for a small stage with limited space offstage. Please adapt your production to make the best use of the space you have available.

The Cat Flap

Act One

SOUND FX: *Before the curtain rises, we hear the sound of occasional* HAMMERING, *like a sculptor chipping at marble. This continues every few moments until Jack Hadley's first entrance. Interspersed with the hammering is the occasional sound of* CATS *in the background.*

SOUND FX: *As the* CURTAIN RISES *'Give Seven' by* The Bill McGuffie Quintet *is playing on the* RADIOGRAM.

MAVIS HADLEY, *the cattery owner, is standing at the kitchen table. A cigarette droops from the corner of her mouth. She is using a large ladle to slop cat food from a large pan into bowls on a wooden tray. A tall pile of bowls stands next to the tray. She carries the tray towards the French doors.*

SOUND FX: *The* TELEPHONE RINGS *as she passes the telephone table.*

LIGHTING FX: *She picks up the phone and without even putting it to her ear she replaces the receiver and continues outside,* TURNING ON THE OUTSIDE LIGHT *at a switch by the French doors, each action almost without stopping.*

MAVIS: (*off*) Here's your food you ungrateful beasts.

SOUND FX: CATS WAIL

MAVIS: (*off*) Wait your turn the rest of you.

SOUND FX:	We hear the CLATTER OF BOWLS being thrown down and more LOUD TAPPING NOISES *coming from the cellar.*

Shortly, MAVIS *re-enters through the French doors.*

SOUND FX:	As she passes the telephone table the PHONE RINGS *again.*

Again, she picks it up and replaces it immediately. She goes back to the kitchen table and places 4 more bowls on the tray and, like an automaton, slops more cat food into them. Her cigarette has burnt down, and she looks about vaguely for an ashtray. Unable to find one, she drops the cigarette butt into the large pan and exits through the French doors again.

SOUND FX:	The PHONE RINGS *yet again as she is passing it and this time she slams the phone down hard.*
LIGHTING FX:	The OUTSIDE LIGHT BUZZES AND GOES OUT.

As MAVIS *exits through the French doors,* JACK HADLEY (SCRATCHY), *her brother, enters DR.*

SOUND FX:	At the same time a radio announcer is heard interrupting the music.

JACK *moves stiffly due to his wooden leg. His right trouser leg, over his wooden leg, is almost in tatters. His face and hands are covered in dust. The spectacles he wears have sticking plaster holding one arm in place. He sits forlornly at the kitchen table and starts to unlace his working boots.*

SOUND FX: **RADIO ANNOUNCER:** News has just come in that President Kennedy has been shot. There's no news yet of his condition. It happened as the President was riding with his wife in an open car through the streets of Dallas, Texas. Several shots rang out and the President collapsed into the arms of his wife. One eyewitness said he saw blood on the President's head. The Governor of Texas, Mr John Connally, who was with him, was also shot down. The President was rushed to hospital, where there's still no word of his condition.

SOUND FX: *As the announcement ends,* MAVIS *enters through the French doors and* TURNS OFF THE RADIO.

SCRATCHY (JACK): Oi, I was listening to that. This is important stuff.

MAVIS: (*taking a couple of clean plates from draining board and putting them away on the kitchen dresser*) We haven't got time for that now. Anyway, you've got them ferals to feed.

SCRATCHY: (*standing*) Did you not hear me woman? The President's bin shot.

MAVIS: (*moving towards the kitchen table*) Yes, well I can think of a few more people round here that could do with being shot.

SCRATCHY: You're a cold-hearted woman, Mavis Hadley. If you weren't my sister....

MAVIS: Yes? (*she picks up the ladle and points it threateningly at* SCRATCHY *- pause*) Nothing to say, Scratchy? Right, well get out there and see to them ferals. (*Slaps ladle into his chest for him to take*) And mind you don't tread on 'em this time. They're worth 5-bob each - if we can find some suckers to take 'em. (*Moves towards the kitchen area.*)

SCRATCHY: (*under his breath as he slops food into bowls*) Cold as an iceberg. (*exits through French doors carrying tray of bowls*)

SOUND FX: *As he exits we hear a* MOTORBIKE PULLING UP *somewhere outside, followed immediately by the sound of a* DOOR OPENING UPSTAIRS *and* 'Please, Please Me' *by* The Beatles *coming from Lulu's bedroom. We* *hear* LULU *starting to run downstairs.*

MAVIS: (*shouting towards the archway*) And you can turn that racket off before you go out!

SOUND FX: We hear LULU *walking back upstairs and the* MUSIC IS TURNED OFF.

SCRATCHY *opens the door to nearest cat pen and gingerly eases his way in – wooden leg first.*

SOUND FX: There is a loud HOWLING AND WAILING OF CATS. *All hell breaks loose inside pen.*

LULU (Louisa): (*bouncing into room. She is young, pretty and fashionable*) You're not my mother, Mavis.

MAVIS: A good job for you I'm not. You're not too old to be put across my knee and given a good spanking. (*She moves to the sink and starts scrubbing at a badly burnt pan*)

SCRATCHY *re-enters through the French doors, dishevelled and breathing heavily, his spectacles askew. He flops down onto one of the kitchen chairs.*

SCRATCHY: Have I ever told you I hate cats?

MAVIS: I don't know why you let 'em use you for a scratch-post, Scratchy. You've got through three wooden legs in the last 10 year.

LULU: (*putting on her lipstick at the mirror above the radio table*) I don't know why you bother with them cats, Dad. You want to get out there and enjoy life instead of being cooped up in here every day with all these smelly old moggies. (*casting a meaningful eye at Mavis*)

MAVIS: I'll have you know it's them cats as brings money into this house, which is more than you or your deadbeat father ever do. And me running around after you both like a skivvy all hours of the day. (*pause*) It's a wonder I haven't worked meself into an early grave.

LULU: (*under her breath*) 'I'm up every morning at the crack of dawn….'

MAVIS: I'm up ev'ry mornin' at the crack of dawn.

LULU: (*under her breath*) '…and what thanks do I get?'

MAVIS: And what thanks do I get?

SOUND FX: A MOTORBIKE HORN *sounds outside.*

LULU: Bye! (*she exits through French doors*)

MAVIS: Sod all. (*to* SCRATCHY) I could murder that daughter of yours sometimes.

SCRATCHY: She thinks highly of you too.

MAVIS: (*pause*) Have you finished sorting out that boiler yet? It's taking you long enough.

SCRATCHY: Well, come down and see for yourself. It's not an easy job. I've got to….

MAVIS: You know I don't like going down there after what happened. It's cold and it's dark and it's got bad memories for me. (*pause*) Just get it sorted before the cold weather comes. I can't live without hot water for ever. (*Gets back to scrubbing the pan again*)

SOUND FX: (under the previous speech) MOTORBIKE DRIVES OFF

COLONEL BULSTRODE PYKE: (*Off*) Damned infernal motorbikes!

SOUND FX: *Loud collective* CAT WAILS

COLONEL: Damned cats! (*enters through French doors carrying a twelve-bore shotgun under his arm*) Bagged a lot of those blighters out in Hyderabad during the Raj. Bigger than these namby-pamby creatures.

MAVIS: What are you doing here?

COLONEL: (*waving an official looking document*) I'm going to get you to sign this damn piece of paper, Mavis, if it's the last thing I do.

SOUND FX: *A* CAT WAILS *off stage.*

The COLONEL *raises his gun to take aim at it waving the shotgun around dangerously.*

MAVIS: It'll be over my dead body when you do. Will you stop waving that gun about?!

SCRATCHY: It'll be loaded I suppose.

COLONEL: Of course it's loaded. What's the use of a shotgun that's not loaded? (*holds it out to* SCRATCHY) Hold this a minute. (SCRATCHY *takes it very gingerly.* COLONEL *slams the document down in the kitchen table and starts rummaging through his*

	pockets.) Where's me damn pen? Get me a pen, Scratchy. Come on. Chop. Chop.
SCRATCHY:	I'm not your batman anymore – Sir.
MAVIS:	For the one hundredth time, Colonel, I am not signing your precious document. You <u>gave</u> me this house - I thought out of the kindness of your heart. Obviously, I was very much mistaken.
COLONEL:	Hmm – I thought it was for services rendered.
MAVIS:	What did you say?! *(Moves away from the sink and takes a step towards the* COLONEL *with a threatening scrubbing brush in her hand)*
COLONEL:	How are you getting on down in that cellar, Scratchy?
MAVIS:	Don't change the subject!
COLONEL:	Now then, Mavis, don't get yourself upset.
MAVIS:	Upset?! Upset?! What have <u>I</u> got to be upset about? You – you – *(she is lost for words. Returns to the sink and attacks the pan again noisily.)*

COLONEL: Shouldn't you be working on that little problem down in the cellar, Scratchy? (*He twitches severely with his head bobbing to the left. This is a nervous tic, which, as we will discover later, is hereditary. He slides a 10/- note into Scratchy's top pocket, without MAVIS seeing, accompanied by a sly wink, which then develops into another nervous tic.*) We might a need a minute or two here.

SCRATCHY: Right you are, Sir. There was a strange white cat down there this afternoon. It might be one of Jean's. (*He hands the gun back to the Colonel having been clearly uncomfortable holding it.*) I'll see if I can get rid of it. (*He disappears quickly down into the cellar (DR), relieved to get away from the impending explosion*)

COLONEL: (*moves towards Mavis*) Now, now, Mavis, let's not have any of this nonsense. We both know that whatever happened between us happened a long time ago.

MAVIS: (*moves towards him again with the brush in her hand*) What we did might have happened when we were much younger, but the evidence of our sins is still with us, Colonel. Living and breathing - and me not allowed to share a part of them. It's not easy for me you know. I might look and sound like a heartless old hag but I'm hurting, Colonel. You've hurt me deep, and if this house is the only consolation I get out of a life of misery and deceit then I'm going to damn well hold on to it.

SOUND FX: *We hear the* CHINK, CHINK *of* SCRATCHY *working in the cellar as* JEAN PALMER *enters through the French doors. The noises continue intermittently throughout the following scene.*

JEAN *is about 60 and dressed almost entirely in tweeds with thick woollen stockings and a tweed cap with a feather in it. She sports a string of pearls throughout the play. If she doesn't look exactly like Margaret Rutherford, the make-up department has done a poor job.*

COLONEL: (*slight pause*) You won't sign today then? (*Mavis raises her scrubbing brush threateningly. The Colonel raises his gun in self-defence.*)

JEAN: Well, what do you think of that then? Another good mystery to solve.

COLONEL: Now put that brush down!

JEAN: (*Seeing the raised brush and the looks on their faces*) Hello – not interrupting you two lovebirds, am I?

MAVIS: Go away. (*JEAN ignores this*)

COLONEL: What are you blithering on about woman?

JEAN: The President. He's been shot.

COLONEL: What President?

JEAN: *The* President. J-F-K. Kennedy.

COLONEL: Don't be stupid. We don't shoot Presidents in this country.

JEAN: In America. The President of the United States.

COLONEL: Well, there you are then. What do you expect? Damn Yankees. Always up to something. Wouldn't happen here.

JEAN: It was some madman with a gun. (*Looks him up and down as though* *it's just occurred to her that it could be him*) There's enough of *them* around here.

Slightly embarrassed, the COLONEL *leans the gun up against the wall next to the cellar door.*

MAVIS: Anything else?

JEAN: Yes – I've reported your nuisance phone calls.

MAVIS: I can do that for myself thank you.

COLONEL: What calls?

MAVIS: None of your business – unless you're going to admit it's been you all the time.

COLONEL: No idea what you're on about, woman.

JEAN: Ooh, it's very dark and exciting. There's a mysterious stranger calling her every hour of the day and night. And he never says a word.

COLONEL: (*suspiciously*) Then how do you know it's a he?

JEAN: It's always a he. We ladies don't do that sort of thing. I'll find out who's at the bottom of it all and flush them out. He'll make a mistake.

	They always do. And when he does, I'll be there to bring him to justice.
MAVIS:	Oh, do shut up, Jean. You sound ridiculous.
COLONEL:	Damned amateur detectives. Ought to be a law against 'em.
JEAN:	I suppose *you'd* have us shot, Colonel Bulstrode Pyke.
COLONEL:	*Have* you shot? I'd damn well do it meself.
JEAN: (*to Mavis*)	Killing, it's ingrained in the male psyche, they can't help themselves. It goes back to the hunter-gatherer in them.
MAVIS & COLONEL: (*in unison*) Oh shut up, Jean!	
SOUND FX:	More TAPPING NOISES *from the cellar.*
JEAN: (*pacing*)	You mark my words, whoever shot the President will be a male psychopath – in his 20's, a Communist I'll wager, fairly well educated, a trained gunman with... (JEAN *stops to listen to the noises emanating from the cellar*) Is that brother of yours still beavering away down in the cellar? Anyone

would think he was searching for buried treasure!

The COLONEL *looks sheepish and begins to whistle for distraction. His twitching resumes.*

MAVIS: (*moves C*)   Jean Palmer, you've been a good friend to this cattery and helped us out now and again, but you do talk a lot of twaddle at times.

VOICES OFF: *The excited voices of two men and a woman can be heard off as* TARQUIN, VERONICA *and* WALTER *enter UR through the cattery area and approach the French doors.* WALTER *is carrying a wicker cat basket.*

VERONICA: What a ghastly little hole! What on earth have you brought me to, Tarquin?

WALTER: (*scolding*)   Mother, really!

TARQUIN *and* WALTER *walk through the doorway first.* TARQUIN *is about 40, a theatrical agent. He looks a little like Clark Gable with dark hair and a thin black moustache.* WALTER *is about 20, thin and wiry with a short-back-and-sides haircut, receding hairline and thick horn-rimmed glasses.*

LIGHTING FX:	*When* VERONICA *enters the* FLICKERING OUTSIDE LIGHT COMES ON *shining brightly, bathing the woman in a warm glow. She stands for a moment like a movie star with screen presence in sharp contrast to her shabby surroundings. She is about 40 and still quite attractive with long flowing blonde hair (rather like Veronica Lake).*
TARQUIN:	Hello Pater.
COLONEL:	Tarquin, my boy? (*He twitches to left. Tarquin responds with an almost identical twitch, bobbing his head to the right.*) What are you doing here? Thought you were in London?
TARQUIN:	London was too busy – and anyway the show closed early. Thought we'd all decamp here to catch some Devon air for a few days. Blow a few cobwebs away.
COLONEL:	And who are 'we'? Are you going to introduce me to this charming young lady?
TARQUIN:	This is my very good friend and leading lady, Veronica. Colonel Alastair Bulstrode Pyke, may I

                                 introduce Veronica Pigeon – and her son, Walter. (WALTER *smiles embarrassedly and wanders to a nearby bookcase where he puts down the basket, inspects the books, picks one up and starts studying it intently.*)

LIGHTING FX: Veronica steps inside and the OS LIGHT GOES OFF immediately.

COLONEL: (*taking Veronica by the hand*) Such a pleasure to meet you, my dear. I get few opportunities to meet Tarquin's theatrical associates these days, but I must say, if they are all as delightful as you, I shall be making my way up to London more often. So, you are appearing in Tarquin's latest venture?

MAVIS: (*tactfully rescuing Veronica from the Colonel's grasp*)   Yes, and I expect she's very tired from her journey. Would you like a cup of tea and a sit down? (*she flicks one of the chairs with a teacloth and dust flies everywhere*)

VERONICA: (*pulling herself free from the* COLONEL)   Not at all. (*reacting to the dust*) Oh. I think I'd rather stand. (TARQUIN

	takes the teacloth from MAVIS *and tries to clean the chair more thoroughly)* I take it you are the owner of this establishment.
MAVIS:	Mavis Hadley. (MAVIS *extends a hand but* VERONICA *ignores it)*
VERONICA:	Walter, give this lady the cat and we can be on our way. His names Her<u>cules</u>. (*pronounced as in Hercules Poirot),* He only eats salmon pate. (*picking up the ladle gingerly and peering at the food attached to it*) I take it you can do that. (WALTER *picks up the basket and hold it out at arm's length to* MAVIS.)
MAVIS:	He'll get our very best attention. Like all our little charges. (*Takes the cat box from* WALTER *and exits through French doors.)*
JEAN:	Did you say your name was Pigeon? Hah. A pigeon among the cats. That's rich.
VERONICA:	(*Registers* JEAN's *presence for the first time. Disdainfully.)* Very amusing. And you are?

JEAN: Jean Palmer. Mavis's oldest friend and next-door neighbour. We are known locally as the mad cat ladies. (*She holds her hand out, but* VERONICA *ignores it.*) And you are....?

COLONEL: That Scarlet Woman!

VERONICA: Are you referring to me?

COLONEL: That Scarlet Woman. That was you. Drury Lane wasn't it.

VERONICA: Oh, I see. Yes, that was me, but – dare I say it, that was a little while ago.

COLONEL: Twenty years at least. Knew I recognized you. I say, didn't we – um – delicate matter – best not....

JEAN: Ooh. Intrigue. A scarlet woman with a shady past.

VERONICA: I think you must be mistaken. I'm sure we've never met before. Walter, I think we should be leaving. Tarquin?

WALTER: Oh, must we go. I was hoping to take a look at this cellar –

TARQUIN: (*stretching his eyes at Walter*) Walter!

WALTER: What?

TARQUIN: Perhaps you're right, Veronica.

COLONEL: (*to* VERONICA) So - to what do we owe the pleasure of your company?

TARQUIN: (*indicating* VERONICA *and* WALTER) I thought I'd bring VW down to see the ancestral pile.

COLONEL: VW? Did you come in a camper van?

JEAN: I think he means Veronica and Walter.

VERONICA: We came by train.

WALTER: The 4:50 from Paddington.

VERONICA: Yes, we've heard so much about the delights of Maydmaster Village and, of course, Maydmaster Manor.

WALTER: So much history - and the legends. Is it true that Cromwell stayed here?

JEAN: Oh, there are so many stories to tell. As Chairlady of the Local History Society, I would be only too pleased to enlighten you.

WALTER: (*with genuine excitement*) Wizard!

COLONEL: The Bulstrode Pykes go way back. We were here long before that upstart Cromwell. The Bulstrode Pykes have fought in every campaign from Agincourt to the Somme, you know.

TARQUIN: And World War II, Pater. Don't forget about my contribution.

COLONEL: ENSA doesn't count. (*to* VERONICA) Flat feet - can't be helped.

TARQUIN: They also serve who only stand in the wings.

VERONICA: Well said, darling! We did our bit for the troops' morale.

COLONEL: (*eyeing up* VERONICA) I'll say. (COLONEL *and* TARQUIN *twitch in unison*)

SOUND FX: *There is a* LOUD CRASH *from the cellar, followed by a* LOUD SPLASH *as* MAVIS *enters through French doors.*

COLONEL: What on earth?!

MAVIS: It's Scratchy, my brother. He's down in the cellar.

VERONICA: Taking a bath?

JEAN: (*moves DR*) I'll go and investigate.

COLONEL: (*following* MAVIS) Er, no, no – I don't think that's a good idea.

VERONICA: Is he naked?

COLONEL: He was mending the boiler.

JEAN: He could be hurt.

COLONEL: Yes, well, all the more reason why you shouldn't go down there. (*he steps in front of the cellar door*)

JEAN: I'm a first aider.

WALTER: I'll come with you. I got a scouting badge for my slings and bandages.

VERONICA: You stay up here, Walter. It'll be all dusty down there. You stay here where it's clean – (*wiping her finger along the top of a chair*) – ish.

COLONEL: There's no need for anyone to go down there. Scratchy's an old soldier. He can look after himself. (*he picks up the gun as he calls down the cellar steps*) You all right down there, Scratchy? (*no response*)   See, nothing wrong.

JEAN: He could be dead!

COLONEL: He won't need any help then, will he?

JEAN: Step aside.

COLONEL: Tarquin, help me out here.

TARQUIN: Yes, Pater. (*He links his left arm under Jean's right arm while the* COLONEL *links his right arm under her left arm and they lift* JEAN *bodily off the floor and frog-march her back towards the kitchen table, her feet paddling wildly. They leave her at the table and take a few steps backwards.* JEAN, *thinking she can get between them, charges towards the cellar door with her arms still flailing. The* COLONEL *and* TARQUIN *scoop her up again. At the same moment* WPC. HASTINGS, *in uniform, enters through the French window carrying* LULU, *struggling, in her arms.*)

WPC. HASTINGS: (*kicking out at an unseen cat*) Get out of the way!

SOUND FX: A CAT WAILS

LULU/JEAN (*together*): Put me down! Let me go!

LULU *and* JEAN *are both unceremoniously dumped into two of the kitchen chairs simultaneously.* TARQUIN *moves DL to join* VERONICA *as if to protect her from the confusion that is going on. She dusts him down, straightens his hair and tie etc.*

so that they are too pre-occupied to see what JEAN *is doing. During the next couple of lines, the* COLONEL *moves stealthily DR to the open cellar door and peers down.* JEAN *follows closely behind him and when the* COLONEL *turns his back to the door, she nips behind him and down the cellar stairs unseen.* WALTER *only has eyes for* LULU *and also does not notice her going.)*

LULU: Ouch! You can't do this to me!

WPC. HASTINGS: It's for your own good.

LULU: You're a pig-headed, mean-spirited busy body. You can't do this to me all the time! (*she starts crying,* WALTER *offers her a clean handkerchief*)

WPC. HASTINGS: You can't talk to me like that. I'm a representative of the law.

LULU: (*taking* WALTER's *handkerchief*) Thank you. (*to* HASTINGS) I'll talk to you any way I like. You're always doing this to me.

JEAN *disappears into the cellar)*

WPC. HASTINGS: What?

LULU: Stopping me from seeing my boyfriends. (*she wails*)

COLONEL: (*moving back C, waving his gun dramatically at HASTINGS*) What have you been up to Hastings?

LULU: She does everything she can to stop me seeing my boyfriends. (*wails louder.*)

WPC. HASTINGS: This is a police matter, Colonel Bulstrode Pyke. I'm not sure if I should….

COLONEL: And I'm a magistrate. If it's a police matter, you'll bring it to me tomorrow anyway.

JEAN PALMER *enters DR from the cellar. She is dishevelled and covered in dust. She immediately exits, unnoticed by anyone else, through the French doors.*

WPC. HASTINGS: Well, Sir. (*takes out her notebook and adopts her official, evidence giving voice*) I was proceeding in a westerly direction along Seaview Terrace when I apprehended Miss Louisa Hadley and a companion…….

COLONEL: Just tell me in your own words, woman.

LULU: This is all a load of nonsense. (*she wails again*)

WPC. HASTINGS: …. a companion riding on a motorcycle, proceeding in a disorderly manner during the hours of darkness…

COLONEL: Cut to the chase, Hastings!

WPC. HASTINGS: I feared for the young lady's safety, sir.

LULU: Rubbish! You just wanted to interfere – like you always do.

WPC. HASTINGS: I feared for her safety as they were riding with a deflective light.

VERONICA: Defective, detective.

LULU: You're pathetic! You just don't like any of my boyfriends. (*she wails even louder than before.*)

JEAN *re-enters through the French doors carrying a long coil of rope over her shoulder. She grabs a large first-aid case from next to the kitchen sink, crosses DR and exits down the cellar stairs. Only* WALTER *pays her any attention.*

WPC. HASTINGS: That's not true.

LULU: What about poor Knuckles?

VERONICA: (*snootily*) He sounds like a real charmer.

WALTER: Mother – do let the poor girl continue.

LULU: (*flutters her Dusty Springfield eyelashes at Walter*) Oh, thank you. At least somebody is on my side.

WALTER: (*totally under* LULU's *spell*) I can't bear to see a young lady in distress.

LULU: My knight in shining armour.

WALTER: Oh, gosh.

VERONICA: Oh God, not love at first sight. Somebody get me a bucket.

MAVIS *enters through the French doors carrying a bucket which she plonks on the kitchen table. Water slops over the table.*

MAVIS: What's going on here? You're making too much noise. You're disturbing the cats.

TARQUIN: (*slight pause*) What happened to poor Knuckles, that's what I want to know?

VERONICA: Who gives a damn?

LULU: (*crying again and pointing at Hastings*) She killed him!

WPC. HASTINGS: I did not. He killed himself.

LULU: (*loudly*) You arrested him and threw him in a cell.

WPC. HASTINGS: (*louder*) He was a kidnapper.

LULU: (*screaming*) He took me on holiday for the weekend.

WPC. HASTINGS: I didn't know he was a claustrophobic! I was only going to keep him in the cell for one night. How was I to know he'd…. (*LULU's loud wailing cuts off any more of his explanation*)

FX: COLONEL BULSTRODE PYKE *lets off one barrel of his shotgun.*

COLONEL: Too much damned noise!

FX: *A light shower of plaster floats down*

SOUND FX. CATS WAIL

MAVIS: (*angry*) That's nice. You've set them all off now It'll take all night to settle them.

SOUND FX/FX: *There is a* LOUD CRASH *and another* SPLASH *from the direction of the cellar. A* CLOUD OF DUST *bursts through the cellar door.*

Everyone looks aghast for a few seconds until JEAN *emerges from the dust.*

JEAN: (*appearing DR at the cellar door. She is even more dishevelled than* *before with her hair in a mess and her skirt torn*) It's – I need – some help.

JEAN *faints dramatically and* HASTINGS *reaches her just in time to stop her falling to the floor. With* TARQUIN *and* WALTER's *help, they drag her to the table and sit her in one of the chairs.* TARQUIN *fans her with a tea towel.* WALTER *pats the back of her hand rather pathetically.*

COLONEL: (*unsympathetically*)   Bring her round. Make her talk.

MAVIS: This is not a gangster movie, Colonel. (*to Tarquin*) Give her some air.

TARQUIN: I am!

MAVIS: Loosen her clothing.

TARQUIN: (*stops fanning*)   I'd really rather not.

COLONEL: Tarquin, just give her a back hander. (*Tarquin raises his hand as if to strike Mavis*)   Not her!

TARQUIN: (*looking at all the women in turn*)   Right oh, Pater, err, which one?

MAVIS: Men! Get out of the way. (MAVIS *gently shakes* JEAN *to wake her but she remains in a stupor*) Wakey, wakey, Jean.

COLONEL: (*pushing MAVIS to one side and grabbing JEAN by the lapels of her tweed jacket he shakes her roughly*) Come on you old trout, wake up!

JEAN: (*waking alarmed and pointing dramatically at the cellar*) He's fallen....

VERONICA: Who?

COLONEL: Scratchy, of course.

JEAN: .... down the well! (*she faints again*)

MAVIS: Well?!

TARQUIN: Not by the look of it.

LULU: We don't have a well.

MAVIS: Don't just stand there, you men. Go and have a look. He could be drowning.

LULU: Drowning?! Oh, Father! (*she faints dramatically*)

WALTER *and* HASTINGS *fight to get the tea towel from* TARQUIN *to fan* LULU. WALTER *wins when* HASTINGS *lets go and falls backwards onto her bottom, ending CL, upstage from* VERONICA.

VERONICA: Ugh! Tarquin – do something about this! (*indicating HASTINGS and the general confusion*)

TARQUIN: (*stepping over* HASTINGS, *who is trying to get up, and pushing her back down on the floor again*)   Oh, my darling. This must be such an ordeal for you. (*He hugs her*)

SOUND FX: *An old-fashioned* DOORBELL RINGS, *long and hard.*

MAVIS: Who on earth can that be? Nobody ever comes to the front door. (*to* COLONEL) Alastair, you go and check on Scratchy. I'll see who it is.

MAVIS exits DL, stepping over HASTINGS and pushing her back to floor once more. The COLONEL exits DR, coughing through the dust. WALTER is on his knees, fanning LULU with the tea towel.

COLONEL: (*off*)   Hadley! Stop messing about man. (*pause*) Have you found anything yet? (*pause*)   Hadley!

The MYSTERIOUS STRANGER, *disguised as* ARCHIE GATHASIT, *enters DL. He is dressed flamboyantly in a floppy felt hat, evening dress under a long back cape with red silk lining and a long white silk scarf which is wrapped around the lower part of his face. He carries a silver-topped cane and is wearing a white wig in a page-boy style. The wig, the hat and the scarf combine to almost completely hide his face but from what we can see he is over made-up to look about 70 years of age.*

MYSTERIOUS STRANGER: ....and I couldn't help noticing your B&B sign so I was hoping you might.... Oh – have I called at a difficult time?

MAVIS: (*entering, flustered, behind him*) Not at all. It's just that a few friends have called in for…. (HASTINGS *has rolled over onto her stomach and is trying to get up again. She steps on her, pushing her down face first onto the floor again.*) …. for….err….

MYSTERIOUS STRANGER: I haven't seen anything like this since Act 5, Scene 2 of Hamlet. (*uses his cane to prod* HASTINGS *bottom back to the floor with a flourish*) Now cracks a noble heart. Good night, sweet prince, and flights of angels sing thee to thy rest. (VERONICA *eyes him with suspicion. To* Mavis) You must be Gertrude.

MAVIS: Mavis.

MYSTERIOUS STRANGER: Ah, Mavis, the sweet sound of the song thrush. It's a pleasure to meet you. (*he extends his cane to* HASTINGS *who uses it to pull herself up*)

TARQUIN: And who might you be?

VERONICA: Have we met before?

MYSTERIOUS STRANGER: Archie Gathasit at your service. (*he bows slightly*) I just happened to be in the area, and I find myself without safe haven for the night. (*to* VERONICA*)* I find I must thrust myself upon your good nature.

VERONICA: Don't look at me. I'm new here. (*indicating* MAVIS) Ask her.

MAVIS: As you can see, we're a busy right now. There's a bit of a crisis going on.

JEAN: (*groggily*) Nnnnngggg…. (*she opens one eye*) ……a mysterious stranger…. (*she faints again*)

Politely, WALTER *starts to rise.*

MYSTERIOUS STRANGER: No don't get up. I can see you have your hands full, fanning the fair Ophelia.

VERONICA: (*suspicious*) Are you sure we haven't met before, Mr...

MYTERIOUS STRANGER: Gathasit, dear lady, Doctor Archie Gathasit - Esquire.

VERONICA: Doctor Who?

MYSTERIOUS STRANGER: No, Doctor Gathasit. Archie Gathasit at your service. (*he bows again*)

TARQUIN: A doctor? You have the air of a theatrical about you. I can spot a thespian anywhere.

MYSTERIOUS STRANGER: I <u>have</u> trodden the boards, 'tis true. (*with a flourish, cupping a hand to one ear*) 'I have heard the chimes at midnight.'

MAVIS: (*unimpressed*) Which explains why you nearly broke my blooming doorbell. Ringing it so hard! So, you want a bed for the night, do you?

MYSTERIOUS STRANGER: If 'tis convenient, dear lady?

MAVIS: 'Convenient's' got nothing to do with it. It's 17/6d a night including your breakfast and 6d extra for a bath. Where's your luggage?

MYSTERIOUS STRANGER: I travel light. He who would travel happily must travel light.

COLONEL: (*off DR*) Tarquin! I need you – and bring that lump of a police constable. She's got no brains so perhaps she'll have some brawn!

WPC. HASTINGS: Here! Have some respect for the law.

TARQUIN: (*pushes HASTINGS towards the cellar door. HASTINGS scowls*) Comin', Pater! (*TARQUIN and HASTINGS exit DR*)

MAVIS: Do you want a cup of tea, Mr Gathasit?

MYSTERIOUS STRANGER: I never partake after 3:00 in the afternoon.

MAVIS: Good. I'll show you your room. There's too much going on here to fiddle-faddle about. (*she exits UR during the following speech*) I hope you've eaten because I've got no time for preparing a meal, breakfast is at 7:30 on the dot…….

MYSTERIOUS STRANGER: (*following MAVIS out, he turns at the arch and gives everyone else another bow with a sweep of his cape. Over the above speech*) Until the morrow. Parting is such sweet sorrow. (*he exits dramatically*)

JEAN: (*who has been coming round slowly*) Who on earth was that?

VERONICA: You may well ask. I'll swear……

LULU: (*who has also come to*) Does it matter? He's a paying guest, and there's few enough of them in these parts.

VERONICA: Oh, so you're back with us too, are you? I've never known such histrionics. You'd think someone had died.

WALTER: Don't be so harsh, mother. She's suffered a terrible trauma.

LULU: My hero.

WALTER: Golly, no, not me. (LULU *and* WALTER *gaze lovingly into each other's eyes*)

VERONICA: If you two lovebirds have quite finished batting eyelashes at each other - will you go and get Tarquin, Walter? I don't want to hang about here any longer than I have to. I'm sure he can't be doing anything in the least bit useful. He would be better employed finding me a warm and comfortable bed for the night.

LULU: We've got a spare cat pen outside if you'd like to stay.

VERONICA: No, we wouldn't. Get moving, Walter.

WALTER: (*gulping*) Yes, rather, mother. (*looking only at LULU*) Are you sure you women folk will be alright unattended, me being the only man and all that?

JEAN: I'm sure we'll survive, young man, now scoot.

WALTER *nervously and slowly walks to the cellar door and hesitates.*

VERONICA: (*sarcastically*) Do be careful, my little man.

WALTER, *having second thoughts on staring down into the cellar.*

LULU: You are so brave.

WALTER: (*renewed courage*) Yes, I am rather. Right-o here goes, last one over the top and all that rot. (*he exits DR*)

JEAN: I should be going with him, of course, but I really don't feel myself yet.

LULU: You've taken a bit of a battering, Jean. I'm sure the men can handle it.

VERONICA: Hah! I've never known a man yet that can handle an emergency.

LULU: Well, they will do their best, I'm sure.

VERONICA: (*to* JEAN, *who is sitting with her head in hands*) Have you looked at yourself in the mirror lately?

JEAN: I suppose I must look a mess. (*She starts to get up but feels faint*)

LULU: Let me help you.

JEAN: You are a dear, Lulu. But you must be feeling a bit groggy yourself.

LULU: I'm fine. I'm a bit younger than you.

VERONICA: And the rest.

LULU: I shall recover quicker than you. (*pointedly, aimed at* VERONICA) Older people need to be treated with love and respect.

JEAN: (*instantly behaving younger and spritelier*) Yes, well don't labour the point, Lulu. (*straightening up in front of the mirror*) I might have a couple of years on you but I'm not in my grave yet. (*she pulls at the cord that operates the wall light over the mirror, but it doesn't come on*)

VERONICA: I think you need to decide whether your dying or not, Jean. I saw a better performance of the dying

JEAN: *(trying the light switch again but without success)* What are you saying?

VERONICA: Just that you seem to have your wits about you rather more than I'd expect for a woman who had serious concussion only two minutes ago.

LULU: So, you're a doctor too, are you?

VERONICA: *(moves UC towards the French doors and takes out a cigarette which she places in a long cigarette holder and lights with an elegant lighter)* I don't have to be a doctor to be observant. Speaking as one actress to another, Jean, you can take in some of the people all of the time, but you can't pull the wool over everyone's eyes.

JEAN: I think you might be mixing your metaphors, my dear. I don't know what you think you know about me, but I am sure there is much less to me than meets the eye.

VERONICA: That would be difficult. *(she leans nonchalantly against the door frame.)*

SOUND/LIGHTING FX:	*The* LIGHTS BUZZ AND FLICKER AND BOTH THE OUTSIDE LIGHT AND THE LIGHT OVER THE MIRROR COME ON AND BATHE THEM IN LIGHT
JEAN:	Not so many years ago, you would have been burnt as a witch.
VERONICA:	It takes one to know one.
LULU:	Are you always this rude?
VERONICA:	You are seeing me at my best.
LULU:	Then it's a good job that you won't be staying long.
VERONICA:	Oh, don't get your hopes up, Louisa. You might be seeing much more of me in the future.
JEAN:	Oh really?
VERONICA:	I thought you fancied yourself as an amateur sleuth. You ought to have worked that out.
JEAN:	It seems you know more about us than we do about you.
VERONICA:	Oh, Tarquin never stops talking about you all. You'd be surprised what I've picked up.

JEAN: I have been wondering what a lady of your background would find of any interest in a backwater like this.

VERONICA: You're right of course. A lady of my breeding —

JEAN: That's not what I meant.

VERONICA: A lady of my breeding must have an ulterior motive. Mine, odd as it might sound, is that I am deeply in love with Tarquin and would follow him to the ends of the earth. Which, as you can see, is precisely what I have done. (LULU *and* JEAN *are open mouthed*) Don't look quite so shocked. Tarquin is a little sweetie. He might not be blessed with an over-abundance of brain cells, but he and I are perfectly suited.

JEAN: We can tell.

VERONICA: And I have every expectation that he has engineered this weekend away to pop a certain question. It could come at any moment.

TARQUIN: (*off*) Veronica!

VERONICA: (*for the benefit of* LULU *and* JEAN)	Yes, my little chocolate soldier! I'm here! (*she moves DR towards the cellar doo.*)
LIGHTING FX:	*The* OUTSIDE AND WALL MIRROR LIGHTS GO OFF INSTANTLY. LULU *and* JEAN *synchronise their eyebrow raising*)
TARQUIN: (*off*)	It's Walter. The boys feeling a bit queasy. Needs his mother's touch.
VERONICA:	What's going on down there?
COLONEL: (*off*)	Bally well come and get this excrescence out of my hair!
WPC. HASTINGS: (*off*)	Is that wise sir. We have enough bodies down here already.
COLONEL: (*off*)	We'll have another one if we don't get this snivelling idiot out the way!
LULU:	Bodies?!
WALTER: (*very muffled - off*)	It's alright, Mumsie. I'm just feeling a little….
SOUND FX:	*There is a* CRASH *off*
VERONICA:	I'm coming, Walter! (*she exits DR quickly*) (*off*) Oh, it's very dark down here.

There is a general confusion of voices, brief improvised dialogue, people bumping into each other etc.

JEAN: What on earth is going on down there? Come on Lulu, help me down the steps. These men are only going to make matters worse. (LULU *takes her arm and guides her out through the door to the cellar DR*) And mind that third step. It's much deeper than all the rest.

MAVIS: (*enters UR slightly breathlessly*) I'm sorry I was so long. The stupid man wouldn't stop talking. How's Scr…… Oh. Where are you all? (*She sees that she is alone and looks this way and that and decides to go out through the French doors first.*)

As she exits the MYSTERIOUS STRANGER *enters UR. He sees that no-one is there and exits DL, looking for* MAVIS. *As that door closes,* MAVIS *enters through French doors and walks quickly towards the door DL. The* MYSTERIOUS STRANGER *enters just as she reaches it.* MAVIS *and the* MYSTERIOUS STRANGER *react with shock as they back into one another.*

MYSTERIOUS STRANGER: Ah, there you, are. Towels?

MAVIS: What?

MYSTERIOUS STRANGER: Towels. (*holding his hands in front of him dramatically*) Will all great Neptune's ocean wash this blood clean from my hand?

MAVIS: (*quickly goes to dresser UL and finds a towel which she all but throws at the MYSTERIOUS STRANGER)* I don't have time for this now. I can't find my brother.

MYSTERIOUS STRANGER: Then I bid you a fond farewell, Madam. (*he exits UR drying his hands on the towel.* MAVIS *exits DL. There is a slight pause. The* MYSTERIOUS STRANGER *enters UR with the towel draped over one shoulder.*) There was just one more thing…. Ah - (*finding no-one in the room, he exits UC through French doors in search of* MAVIS.)

There is a slight pause before he enters again UC and heads towards the door DL. MAVIS *enters DL just as he reaches the door, and they repeat their shocked meeting.*

MAVIS: What the….!! (*clutching at her heart*) Are you a doctor or an undertaker? Anyone would think you were trying to drum up business?

MYSTERIOUS STRANGER: Flannel.

MAVIS:	Yes, I know. You're full of it.
MYSTERIOUS STRANGER:	A face flannel, if I may, and then you may rest in peace.
MAVIS:	If only. (*she goes to dresser and gives him a flannel. She watches to make sure he exits UR before moving DR to the cellar door.*) Hey ho. Take a deep breath, Mavis. He must be still down there. (*she peers down the cellar steps and calls out tentatively*) Scratchy. (*pause*) You still down there? (*silence*)
LIGHTING FX:	*All the* LIGHTS FLICKER *and* BUZZ
MAVIS:	Is anybody there? (*pause*) Hello, what are <u>you</u> doing there? (MAVIS steps inside the cellar DR)
LIGHTING FX:	The LIGHTS FLICKER *yet again and then* BLACKOUT. *There is a* SCREAM.
SOUND/LIGHTING FX:	A CAT WAILS. *The* OUTSIDE LIGHT FLICKERS *again as the stage falls into* DARKNESS.

CURTAIN

END OF ACT ONE

Act Two

SOUND FX: I Want to Hold Your Hand *by The Beatles*

As the curtain rises the radio plays the Christmas number one single 'I Want to Hold Your Hand' by The Beatles. The French doors are closed. Beyond, snow can be seen falling, adding to what is already laying on the ground. To the front of the raised kitchen area stands a rather pathetic specimen of a Christmas tree which has been poorly adorned with tinsel and assorted baubles. An ancient 'fairy' with a bent wand leans precariously from the top of the tree. A home-made paper chain, that has probably seen 20 years' use, has been stretched haphazardly at ceiling height along the wall R. A two-bar electric fire has been turned on and placed along the R wall upstage from the cellar door. JEAN PALMER *sits alone at the table, writing, pausing to ponder then, smiling, continues to write, pleased with her task.*

SOUND FX: **RADIO DJ:** You don't need me to tell you that was The Beatles with the Christmas number one single and 'I Want to Hold Your Hand'. Well, if you do want to hold hands, you'll need gloves on if you're venturing outside. The snow continues to fall all over the country and the weathermen tell us it will only get worse. So, what could be better

	than Peter, Paul and Mary with 'Blowin' in the Wind'. *(music starts)*
SOUND FX:	JEAN *scoffs, stands, crosses to radiogram, and* TURNS IT OFF. *She stands looking out of the French doors and shivers at what she sees.*
LIGHTING FX:	BRIGHT LIGHTS OF VEHICLE HEADLIGHTS *draw her attention OS.* LIGHT GOES AWAY *as* SCRATCHY, *assisted by* LULU *and* HASTINGS *approach the French doors.* JEAN *opens the doors for them.*
SOUND FX:	WIND HOWLING
JEAN:	Come in, come in. You poor things; you must be frozen to the very marrow.

SCRATCHY *has his right arm in plaster which is held above his head making it awkward for him to manoeuvre, and for those near him as he turns or move etc.*

LULU:	Mind how you go, Dad, you don't want to bang your... (SCRATCHY *bangs raised hand against door frame*) ... hand again.
JEAN:	Poor man. Sit yourself down.

WPC. HASTINGS: What with Mavis an' all. Terrible business. He's lucky to be alive after all 'e's been through.

LULU: (*sarcastically, removing Scratchy's coat*) Yes, thank you for that. It's your cheery good humour that keeps us all going.

WPC. HASTINGS: Sorry I wasn't thinking.

JEAN: Never mind. Let's get Scratchy comfortable.

LULU: That won't be easy.

SCRATCHY *is led to the table where he is plonked down onto a chair. The man sits staring into space vacantly. The others stand and look at him with varying degrees of pity.* LULU *hangs her and Scratchy's coats on hooks at the bottom of the stairs.*

WPC. HASTINGS: He's not a well man, is he? I think they've sent him home too soon. It's too much for a man to bear. Falling down a well, his sister falling down the cellar stairs and breaking her... (*registers that* LULU *is staring at him*) Oh God, sorry.

LULU: Do you get special training in the police force to deal with people's grief?

JEAN: A cup of tea, that's what everyone needs. It'll pep us all up.

LULU: Oh yes, the British answer to all problems, a nice cup of tea.

JEAN: If you'd rather not?

LULU: (*apologetically*) That will be fine...thank you.

JEAN *walks UL to the kitchen area and puts a kettle on the stove.* HASTINGS *picks up Jean's notes from the kitchen table and scans them quizzically.*

JEAN: (*pleased, seeing* HASTINGS *reading her notes*) Ah, I see I am undone, Constable.

WPC. HASTINGS: What is all this exactly?

JEAN: A list.

WPC HASTINGS: I can see that, but what does it all mean?

JEAN: Suspects and motives.

WPC. HASTINGS: For what?

JEAN: (*assured*) Why, murder of course.

SCRATCHY *seems to come out of his trance-like state and stares hard at Jean.* LULU *looks at the woman open mouthed and* HASTINGS *flounders like a stranded fish.*

LULU: What murder?

JEAN: (*moves down to table*) Mavis, obviously.

LULU: Auntie Jean!

WPC. HASTINGS: Misadventure, they said, not murder. You can't go making malicious allegations, Jean. You'll get yourself into all sorts of trouble.

JEAN: (*moving towards the table*) Nonsense. It's all about MOM.

LULU: Mavis was not my mother.

JEAN: Not Mum – MOM. (*Listing them on her fingers*) Means, opportunity, motive. It's like algebra. Find two of them and you can usually work out the other one. 'X' plus 'X' equals 'Y' – but it's not the 'why' that bothers me. I've made a long list of possible motives. She wasn't a well-liked woman. The means is obvious but the opportunity – that's the tricky bit.

LULU: Stop it, Jean. That's horrid. Mavis wasn't murdered. It was just an accident.

WPC. HASTINGS: That's right, Jean. Don't go looking for mysteries where they don't exist. There was a power cut, and she lost her footing in the dark. It could have happened to any one of us.

JEAN: But it didn't, did it? It happened to Mavis. And who would want to kill Mavis?

WPC. HASTINGS: Exactly.

JEAN: (*picking up her list and waving it in front of her*) Almost everybody, that's who. (*drops list back on the table*)

SCRATCHY: (*angrily*) Shut up, Jean

JEAN: Scratchy, you dear man! You've come back to us!

SCRATCHY: She might not have been the nicest person to know at times, but Mavis Hadley would never harm a hair on anyone's head. She had a hard life – mostly devoted to looking after me and Lulu...

WPC. HASTINGS: (*with disdain*) And her blessed cats.

SCRATCHY: Aye – and her cats. And you don't do that unless you've got a kind heart. You should be ashamed of yourself, Jean. I know it's a hobby of yours to be a super-sleuth, but you should think of how much you're hurting other people.

JEAN: You've changed your tune. The number of times I've heard you say you'd swing for that woman. You must have hit your head very hard falling down that well. (*moves back to the kitchen*)

WPC. HASTINGS: (*putting her hand on SCRATCHY's shoulder reassuringly*) I don't think the coroner was worried that you had anything to do with it. There were enough witnesses to say you were unconscious at the bottom of the well.

LULU: (*sitting next to* SCRATCHY) Tell us what happened down there, Dad. I know some of it came out at the inquest, but you weren't well enough to give your evidence.

SCRATCHY: I was hoping you'd all tell me. One minute I was digging, the next I'm falling. I thought I was a goner. I should have been more careful. After all, I knew damn well that damned well was damn well there.

LULU: Did you? I didn't.

SCRATCHY: You'd have been a toddler at the time, Lulu. Do you remember, Jean? It was when we blocked off your

	end of the cellar and put that cat flap in so our cats could come and go between the two houses. Mavis thought the well was dangerous with a little 'un in the house so we boarded it over. See, we'd already lost a cat or two down that well and we didn't want to take any chances.
LULU:	But I've been going down there all my life. I've never seen anything.
SCRATCHY:	There was nothing to see. I'd dug in some old boards over the top of the well. I used some of the stones to lay over the top and bedded them in. Over the years it's just blended in. I'd forgotten it was there. I suppose the boards had rotted and where I was chipping away at the floor it just all gave way.
WPC. HASTINGS:	So why were you digging there in the first place?
SCRATCHY:	Well, that's another story.
LULU:	And...?
SCRATCHY:	I've been sworn to secrecy.
LULU:	Now you're scaring me, Dad. Mavis is dead. Your own sister. My aunty. I

SCRATCHY: think I deserve an explanation if no-one else does.

SCRATCHY: I don't suppose it matters much now. No – I don't care who knows now. (*pause*) I was - looking for something.

JEAN: That's stating the obvious, Scratchy. What were you looking for?

SCRATCHY: (*struggling with his conscience*) Jewels, money – stuff like that.

WPC. HASTINGS: Buried treasure?

SCRATCHY: I suppose you'd call it that. The Colonel says there's a hoard of treasure somewhere down in our cellar; hidden by one of his ancestors in the Civil War. He said if I could find it, he'd let me have a reward and we'd be allowed to stay here. If not (*pause*) he was going to throw us out.

LULU: Throw us out?! What – all of us? Me too?

WPC. HASTINGS: And you never did find it.

LULU: So that's why you were always down there. We thought you were

	just mending the boiler but really you were digging for treasure.
WPC. HASTINGS:	And the Colonel <u>knew</u> you hadn't found it.
JEAN:	Watch out everyone. I think W.P.C. Hastings is having one of her thinking turns. (*to* HASTINGS) Did you know that the Colonel kept asking Mavis to sign this house back to him?
LULU:	Now what are you talking about? This is <u>our</u> house.
SCRATCHY:	It used to be the Colonel's. It's in the grounds of the Manor and always has been. Hundreds of years ago there was a passageway that led from the old Manor House to this Longhouse. But of course, the old Manor House burnt down 200 years ago and when they built the new one the old passageway was lost.
JEAN:	And the Longhouse was divided into our two cottages at the same time - to make farmers' cottages. I expect the well provided water for both properties, which is why the cellar wasn't divided up at the same time.

WPC. HASTINGS: *(slowly)* And Mavis wouldn't sign the house over to him. (*she takes out her notebook, licks her pencil and laboriously starts to make some notes*)

JEAN: (*moves back to the table with a tray of teas*)   Do I see the long arm of the law stretching out its tenacious hand?

WPC. HASTINGS: I think I might need to talk to the Colonel. (*moves DL scribbling notes*)

FX: SNOW STARTS TO FALL OUTSIDE

JEAN: (*puts tray down on table and picks up the list*)   You might, but when you start thinking about opportunities you need to know that when Mavis fell down the stairs (*reading*) the Colonel was at the top of the well, tied to a rope and hauling Scratchy up from a watery death. (*drops list on table*) Not the actions of a murdering, gold-hungry psychopath if you ask me. (HASTINGS *scratches out the notes she has just written.* JEAN *moves back to the kitchen.*)

OS excited voices approach. TARQUIN, *the* COLONEL, WALTER *and lastly* VERONICA, *who carries a raised umbrella, walk toward the French doors.* TARQUIN *pounds a fist on the door.* LULU *opens the door.*

SOUND FX/FX:	WIND HOWLING – SNOW FALLING MORE HEAVILY
LIGHTING FX:	*The three men ungallantly enter first. As* VERONICA *stands in doorway lowering her umbrella and shaking off the snow the OUTSIDE LIGHT FLICKERS on and bathes her in a warm glow, she stands for a moment as a movie star might crave adulation.*
TARQUIN:	Do get in V, its penguin weather, brrr!
WALTER:	Yes, come along, Mumsy.
COLONEL:	Hardly any bally heat in here either. The Manor's as cold as a witch's backside. Boiler packed up wouldn't you know. These things always seem to happen on Christmas Eve. No chance of getting a plumber out until the New Year, I don't suppose.

When the COLONEL *starts talking,* HASTINGS *begins taking notes as if she is trying to take down everything that is being said.*

LIGHTING FX: OS LIGHT GOES OFF *as* VERONICA *moves away from French doors.*

VERONICA: Well, I simply must get warm. (*moving towards the electric fire, she props the umbrella against the wall DR in the same position that the* COLONEL *had propped his gun in act one*)

TARQUIN: (*chuckles and slips an arm around* VERONICA's *waist pulling her toward him*) I can help there.

COLONEL: Now then my boy, steady on. Wait till lights out. (*He twitches to left.* TARQUIN *responds with an almost identical twitch, bobbing his head to the right and they share a lascivious chuckle.*)

VERONICA: (*stands in front of fire to warm herself*) Oh God, we're not staying here all night, are we?

LULU: No one invited you.

COLONEL: If I might say, this house is now my property, again. If anyone needs an invitation, it's you.

LULU: Says who?

COLONEL: The law young lady, the law.

JEAN: Well, the law has not exactly covered itself with glory up to now. (HASTINGS *looks up briefly and then plants a large full-stop to her notepad and puts it back in her top pocket*)

TARQUIN: Meaning what, Miss Palmer?

WPC. HASTINGS: (*holds aloft Jean's notes and shakes them for all to see*) Our lady 'detective' here believes we have a murderer in our midst. (*Just as before when murder is mentioned the entire cast, except* JEAN *stare hard at the constable, falling instantly attentive.*) And you and I, Colonel, need to have a very serious conversation.

COLONEL-WALTER-TARQUIN-VERONICA: Murder?! (*The* COLONEL, TARQUIN, *and* WALTER *twitch to left, right and upwards respectively in unison*)

JEAN: Just so.

COLONEL: (*derisory*) The old trout's still banging on about that shooting in America a month back. Get over it!

JEAN: I agree that the Kennedy assassination has elements of doubt concerning the verdict and identity of the killer, but if I may blow my own trumpet, I did predict his age and political persuasion pretty much spot on.

The COLONEL sighs and raises his hands in disgust. Tarquin leers as Veronica bends over the heater.

TARQUIN: I'm sensing a 'but' here.

JEAN: Just so and a very big but indeed. But – this murder is very much closer to home.

SCRATCHY: Be careful what you say, Jean.

WALTER: Oh, by George, Mr Hadley. I didn't realise you were out of hospital. Welcome home. (*he clumsily tries to shake* SCRATCHY's *left hand with his left hand but, realising this feel's wrong, he swaps to his right hand which then changes into a high-five against the hand emerging from* SCRATCHY's *plastered arm*)

SCRATCHY: Ow!

WALTER: Sorry.

COLONEL: Yes, yes, Scratchy. Welcome home. Should've said it before. Remiss.

LULU: Make your mind up. Is this our home or yours?

WALTER: Please allow me to elucidate.

LULU: If you must.

WALTER: (*trying to sound sympathetic and helpful but only succeeding in sounding pompous*) On the demise – on the unfortunate demise of your aunt, Mavis Hadley, the agreement that transferred this property to her, for her lifetime, was terminated. In a technical and quite legal sense, this property has reverted to the ownership of Colonel Bulstrode Pyke. The Colonel, of course, has no wish to see either you or Mr Hadley made homeless, and he is perfectly happy for you both to stay here until such time as you can find alternative accommodation.

LULU: Alternative….?!

SCRATCHY: What….?!

LULU: What did you say, Jean? Not the actions of a murdering, gold-hungry psychopath? You might have to think again!

HASTINGS *retrieves her notebook from her top pocket, licks her pencil and starts taking more notes.* VERONICA *and* TARQUIN *begin to quietly show an unusual interest in the walls.* TARQUIN *produces a tape measure which he and* VERONICA *use. They stand and muse, pointing, heads close in quiet conversation.*

JEAN: (*seemingly quite happy about the rising level of intrigue and ill-humour*) I'll get some more tea and call you a plumber, Colonel. (*moves to the kitchen area where she busies herself with cups, saucers, teapot etc.*)

COLONEL: What? No chance - time of year - weather conditions - not a cat in hell's chance of getting a plumber - but try if you must.

WALTER: (*shyly*) And how are you doing, Lulu? If I might call you, Lulu?

LULU: Oh, you are sweet, thanks for asking. It's all been a bit of a trial...

WPC. HASTINGS: (*writing*) 'Trial'...sorry, force of habit.

WALTER: Has it been beastly?

LULU: (*fighting back tears*) Yes.

JEAN: Not so beastly that it's stopped you from jaunting about with your

LULU: (*defensive*) It's Nosher – and that's very unfair of you, Jean; life must go on.

SCRATCHY: (*staring dead ahead*) Not for Mavis though, eh. (*pause, to* WALTER) What are you doing here again young man? Staying at the Manor for Christmas?

WALTER: (*sits at the table opposite Scratchy*) Oh no – well, mother and Tarquin just came down today to stay for Christmas. I live here now.

LULU *notices what* VERONICA *and* TARQUIN *are doing and is puzzled.* VERONICA *and* TARQUIN *exit DL still intent on measuring and exchanging whispered comments.*

SCRATCHY: Here?

WALTER: At the Manor. Colonel Bulstrode Pyke has employed me as his secretary.

SCRATCHY: Really?

COLONEL: When it comes to anything practical, he's less use than a chocolate teapot, but put a pen in his hand or ask him to tally up a row of figures and the

	boy's a genius. (*He twitches to the left*)
WALTER: (*embarrassed*)	Oh I say. (*pause – he twitches, shooting his head backwards*) We've just started working on the Colonel's memoirs. (SCRATCHY *looks quizzically at the* COLONEL)
COLONEL:	Exploits in the war, big-game huntin' – ancient family history. That kind of thing.
WALTER:	It's absolutely fascinating.
SCRATCHY:	And will Mavis make an appearance in these memoirs?
COLONEL: (*looking uncomfortable, nervous tic*)	Friends and neighbours will no doubt get a – an appropriate mention – in passing.
SCRATCHY:	I'll not want her memory sullied – if you know what I mean.
COLONEL:	No, no, of course not, Scratchy – of course not.
SCRATCHY:	Proper respect.
COLONEL:	For all concerned.

VERONICA *and* TARQUIN *enter DL and start measuring the wall again.*

WALTER: I say. If we are all going to be here together for the duration, Colonel, you could relate some of your experiences for us. That would be wizard.

SCRATCHY: I'm in no mood for camp-fire stories. This isn't a boy scout jamboree, you know.

WALTER: Oh.

LULU: (*indignantly to* VERONICA *and* TARQUIN) What are you two doing, exactly?

VERONICA *and* TARQUIN *stop their measuring etc and pretend nothing has happened.*

TARQUIN: Nothing. (*twitches*) Just daydreaming, that's all, nothing to worry your pretty self over. (*pats Lulu on the head*

VERONICA: (*unsympathetic – to* TARQUIN) Things will be very different here one day soon but for now this is going to be a Christmas to remember and make no mistake.

LULU: What do you mean?

TARQUIN: Steady on V.

VERONICA: Well, I'm sorry, but it has to be said. They're sitting on a little gold mine here but look what they've done to the place. It's ghastly and the people here are so... (*realising that everyone is watching and listening.*)

JEAN: Oh, do go on my dear. We're all ears. Tell us exactly what you think of us down here - in our little, rural backwater. (JEAN *brings tray with 4 more cups to the table, puts the cups on the table and goes back for milk and sugar.*)

VERONICA: I was merely...forget it.

SCRATCHY: I'd like to know.

LULU: (*folds arms defiantly*) Me too!

VERONICA: Must you all be so bloody melodramatic?!

SCRATCHY: (*struggling, he stands*) My sister has died - possibly murdered.

WPC. HASTINGS: Quite. And when a murder is announced, I need to take statements.

COLONEL: Well, write this down...Poppycock! (*He twitches to the left.* HASTINGS *starts to write it t down then crosses it out again)*

TARQUIN: This is a bit rich! I mean to say, the woman fell, end of story. (*he twitches to the right*)

WALTER: Or was she pushed? (*everyone looks at him – he twitches nervously*) As they say in all the best crime novels.

The COLONEL, TARQUIN, *and* WALTER *all twitch at the same time.*

VERONICA: (*to* JEAN)   Happy now?

LULU *persuades* SCRATCHY *to sit again.*

TARQUIN: Calm down sweetheart.

VERONICA: (*loudly under breath*)   I could easily push the lot of them down the stairs.

JEAN: Write that down, constable.

VERONICA: You dare.

JEAN: Threatening an officer of the law.

HASTINGS *puffs out her chest and slowly strides around the room.*

WPC. HASTINGS: (*turning sharply for effect on Veronica who is unimpressed*)   We'll start with you Miss, if you please. Where

	were you at the time Mavis Hadley snuff...met her untimely death?
VERONICA:	Oh, for God's sake!

JEAN: (*putting milk and sugar down on the table - surprisingly upbeat*) I'll phone that plumber for you, Colonel. (*she moves UR, picks a card from a letter rack next to the radiogram and dials a number*)

VERONICA:	I was down in the cellar. As we all were. (*to* HASTINGS) You included.
WPC. HASTINGS:	But it was very dark down there. There's only one 40-watt bulb and that was covered in cobwebs. It was difficult to make out who was where and who was doing what to whom.
JEAN:	It sounds like one of your discos, Lulu. (*into phone*) Yes, hello, is that (*peering at card in her hand*) Norm? No?
WPC. HASTINGS:	I need to establish exactly where everyone was when the lights went out and Mavis fell down the stairs. So, Miss Pigeon –
VERONICA:	Mrs.

WPC. HASTINGS:	<u>Mrs</u> Pigeon. Exactly where were you when the lights went out and Mavis fell down the stairs?
VERONICA:	I don't know. It was dark.
PC. HASTINGS:	<u>Before</u> the lights went out.
JEAN: (*into phone*)	Oh, hello Norm. Jean Palmer.
VERONICA:	I haven't the faintest idea.
COLONEL:	What is the point of all this? None of us can possibly be suspected of anything. Mrs Pigeon hadn't even met Mavis until 20 minutes before she died. The woman was a tartar but even she couldn't work a complete stranger into a murderous frenzy in 20 minutes!
TARQUIN:	It would take at least half an hour.
JEAN: (*into phone*)	Yes, yes, and Seasons Greetings to you and your good lady wife too. We have a little problem. Two actually. The boilers have gone kaput at the cattery and at Maydmaster Manor. (*pause*) Kaput – defunct – gone belly-up? Yes, yes – not working. (*pause*) Well, I was hoping you could pop out and fix them? (*she moves the phone away*

	from her ear very quickly) I don't think it's funny. Yes, I know it's Christmas Eve. Snowing?
SOUND FX/FX:	*She opens the French doors and there is now a* BLIZZARD OUTSIDE *the* WIND HOWLS. *She slams the door quickly.*
JEAN:	Yes, it is snowing – a bit – here too. We'd be very grateful if you could – what's that? – call out fee – yes, yes, I understand – and double-time for Christmas Eve? – well, I suppose... (*she looks at the* COLONEL *for guidance*)
COLONEL:	Yes, yes, whatever it takes. We can't all spend the whole of Christmas huddled round a two-bar fire.
JEAN: (*into phone*)	Yes – whatever you say, Norm. (*slight pause*) Only maybe? But – (*resigned*) OK. Do what you can. (*she puts the phone down*) And a very merry Christmas to you too.
LULU: (*shivering*)	Is Norm on his way? (*moves to kitchen area and searches for a biscuit barrel in the cupboards*)

JEAN: No, but he's just taken on some new chap who might call in on his way home – if he doesn't get cut off by the snowstorm on the way.

WPC. HASTINGS: (*clears her throat*) As I was saying – I need to establish exactly where everyone was at the time of the alleged….

COLONEL: Shut up, Hastings. You sound ridiculous.

WALTER: I was halfway down the well; it couldn't have been me. Well, to be more precise, I was halfway *up* the well, having already been lowered all the way down once. You see…

TARQUIN: (*cutting off* WALTER *before he sinks into a lengthy, pointless explanation*) And the rest of us were all hanging on to the other end of the rope.

LULU: (*returning with biscuit barrel, which she places on the table*) Except the mysterious stranger, of course,

SCRATCHY: What mysterious stranger?

LULU: Mr. Gathasit, the ham actor fellow

COLONEL: I'd forgotten all about him.

WALTER: Yes, of course. Archie Gathasit. What happened to him?

SOUND/LIGHTING FX: DOORBELL RINGS *which appears to cause a* BLACKOUT. EVERYONE *looks rather stunned and confused toward direction of doorbell while the lights splutter.* BLACKOUT *causes first* VERONICA*, then* LULU *and finally* WALTER *to scream.* WALTER *is screaming as the* LIGHTS COME BACK ON *leaving him feeling rather silly.*

TARQUIN: Who on earth could that be?

VERONICA: (*flatly*) I don't know, I'm not psychic.

No-one moves.

SOUND/LIGHTING FX: DOORBELL RINGS AGAIN *and the* LIGHTS SPLUTTER *again.*

COLONEL: Well, someone bally well answer it.

LULU: (*sarcastic*) Why don't you? It's your house.

SCRATCHY: Now then girl, no need to be rude to the Colonel, he's always been good to us.

LULU *looks flabbergasted at her father.*

WALTER: (*unconvincingly*) Shall I go and see who it is?

VERONICA: (*smiling*) Best not, darling, it could be the killer.

TARQUIN: Actually, all joking aside...

JEAN: So now you start to believe me.

WPC. HASTINGS: I suppose I should go.

They all remain waiting. Apprehensive.

SOUND FX: DOORBELL RINGS AGAIN LONGER AND LOUDER.

COLONEL: Impatient type by the sound of it. Damned impertinence.

SCRATCHY: (*attempts to stand*) If they have to wait much longer, they'll freeze to death.

LULU *and* WALTER *force* SCRATCHY *to sit again.*

LULU: I'll go.

WALTER: No, no, I'll go. (*he twitches nervously*)

JEAN *saves them all the bother and stomps off in positive mood.*

JEAN: Oh, for goodness' sake. Let's wear the old ones out first.

JEAN *opens door DL and exits closing the door behind her.* ALL *lean in trying to hear. There is a mumbled, frustratingly indecipherable conversation which causes cast to rush to listen at the closed door. Poor* SCRATCHY *is left struggling to join them but gives up.*

COLONEL: (*whose hearing is worse than the others*) Who is it?

TARQUIN: Shush, Pater.

WALTER: (*excited*) It's just like one of those old-fashioned Christmas games.

LULU: (*unimpressed*) Oh yes, that well-known children's pastime, 'Is there a sadistic killer at the door?' - very seasonal.

WALTER: (*who is now being squashed between* HASTING *[uncomfortably from behind] and* LULU *[rather pleasantly] from the front*) No – sardines.

There is more murmuring from the hall, and they ALL *try to squeeze even close to the door.* WALTER *squeaks.* SCRATCHY *rises in another attempt to join them.* VERONICA *peels herself off from the back of the crowd, sighs boredly and walks back to warm herself by the two-bar fire.*

TARQUIN: (*nearest the door - panic*) Heads up, they're coming in!

In their haste to assume positions of normality they turn, sending SCRATCHY *and* HASTINGS *tumbling to the floor in a tangled heap.*

SCRATCHY: Mind the arm, you blithering idiot!

TARQUIN *rushes to be beside* VERONICA, *the* COLONEL *stands stiffly with a military bearing,* LULU *and* WALTER *sit together on the edge of the table swinging their legs like naughty children. Door DL opens.* JEAN *enters and stares about the room incredulous.* SCRATCHY *is sprawled on his back in front of the table, struggling with his wooden leg and plastered arm like an upturned tortoise.* HASTINGS *is lying face down on the floor, in the same position as he had been when* ARCHIE GATHASIT *entered.* JEAN *enters DL.*

TARQUIN: Well?

JEAN: I don't know. I can't understand a word he's saying.

JEAN *steps aside, and a middle-aged man dressed in traditional German clothing [with feathered hat, decorated braces and lederhosen]) enters behind her. He sports a large, white moustache which hides half his face. It is the* MYSTERIOUS STRANGER, *in the guise of* ERICH THAAARGIST. *He has no coat, and his head and shoulders are covered in snow. His bare knees are shivering, he is beating his arms to try to get warm and his teeth are chattering making his thick German accent almost impossible to decipher.*

MYSTERIOUS STRANGER: Goot eberning. (JEAN *shrugs*) Mein name ist Erich Thaaargist!!! (*clicking heels together sharply and bowing head, he struggles to resist raising a Nazi* *salute, forcing his right arm down with his left.)*

TARQUIN: *(queries)* Thaaaaaaaargist?

MYSTERIOUS STRANGER: *(goose-stepping over the prostrate* HASTINGS*)* Nein dumbkopf, too many A's. I said Thaaargist. *(softer)* Only three A's.

COLONEL: *(incensed)* He's a bally Kraut! Bloody cheek!

LULU: Live and let live, Colonel. The wars been over for some time now.

COLONEL: I'm fetching me gun to be on the safe side. *(picking up Veronica's umbrella by mistake and pointing it at the* MYSTERIOUS STRANGER*)* Where is it? I left it here when thingy fell down the... *(*MYSTERIOUS STRANGER *steps back over* HASTINGS *in his haste to put some distance between himself and the Colonel)*

SCRATCHY: *(hurt and struggling to get up on his own)* Mavis, my sisters name is...was Mavis.

JEAN: Your precious gun is where you left it - on the shelf by the boiler, down in the cellar.

COLONEL *moves toward cellar door.*

WALTER: Need any help?

COLONEL: No, I'll do it meself. (*Looking back towards the* MYSTERIOUS STRANGER) The air in this room has become unbreathable. (*Exits DR still carrying the umbrella*)

WALTER: Actually, I meant you, Mr Hadley.

WALTER *helps* SCRATCHY *to his feet and to a seat, hurting his arm in process causing* SCRATCHY *to scowl and grumble under his breath.*

VERONICA: Have we met, Mr Thaaargist?

MYSTERIOUS STRANGER: (*shakes head vigorously and goosesteps over the prostrate floundering* HASTINGS) Nein mein frauline! I am, how you zay, new to vis neck of ze voods.

JEAN: You're not the plumber by any chance; the one Norm recommended?

MYSTERIOUS STRANGER: Norm? (*then realising he can grab at this opportunity*) Plum<u>b</u>er? Wass ist this plum<u>b</u>er? Oh ja, ja, Thaaargist ist plum<u>b</u>er!

WALTER:	I say how spiffing. So jolly continental.
VERONICA:	And so fast. We've barely put the phone down.
MYSTERIOUS STRANGER:	I vos in ze areas. (*suddenly aggressive*) Ist zat a crime?! Am I to be hounded all ze days of mein life for vot is happened in ze fatherland?

They are all rather afraid of this strange excitable man.

JEAN:	Well, we are most grateful to you for coming out on such a foul and inclement night.
MYSTERIOUS STRANGER: (*morose*)	Zis ist nuzzing compared to Stalingrad.
JEAN:	I've just made a pot of tea, would you like some?
MYSTERIOUS STRANGER:	Danker shun. (*he bows*)
WALTER:	I say, are you any good with electrics? This house needs some attention before it blows us all up.

MYSTERIOUS STRANGER: Niet – ze electricals are not for ze Thaaargist. I am ze plum<u>b</u>er. I plum<u>b</u>.

TARQUIN: I didn't hear your van when you arrived.

MYSTERIOUS STRANGER: Vot?! Oh nein, nein. Mein van ist broken down, stuck in ze snow - kaput.

JEAN: Just like our boilers.

TARQUIN: It must be a big van.

MYSTERIOUS STRANGER: Vot?

TARQUIN: (*chuckling*) To get your name on the side. (*extends arms very wide*) Thaaaaaaaaaarrrrgist!

VERONICA *laughs like a horse,* WALTER *joins in.*

VERONICA: How witty, darling.

WALTER: Simply splendid, Tarquin.

MYSTERIOUS STRANGER *is angered and begins goose stepping around the room, turning he steps over* HASTINGS *again.*

MYSTERIOUS STRANGER: Zat's right, laugh, but I will have ze last laugh, I will not be fixing your stinking plum<u>b</u>ing!

JEAN *helps* HASTINGS *to her feet. She dusts herself off, straightens her hair, coughs and stands before the* MYSTERIOUS STRANGER, *eying him up and down, both eye one another together up and down.*

TARQUIN: Sorry, old chap. (*he twitches to the right*)

WALTER: Yes, no harm meant. (*he twitches upwards*)

WPC. HASTINGS: If you are a plumber I'll eat my hat.

MYSTERIOUS STRANGER: (*hands his hat to* HASTINGS) Haff mein.

JEAN: Now, now, I'm sure we can all be friends. Let's have a little entente cordiale.

MYSTERIOUS STRANGER: (*coldly*) I vould prefer ze tea.

COLONEL: (*entering DR*) He's still here then. (*to Thaargist, waving his shotgun threateningly*) Watch yourself, young man. None of your funny business. I'm keeping a close eye on you. Now march

JEAN: yourself down into that cellar and start cranking up that boiler.

Now then, Colonel, don't get carried away. We're all friends now. He's not your enemy anymore. (*she hands a cup of tea to the MYSTERIOUS STRANGER*)

COLONEL: I didn't spend all my life in the army fighting for this country just to have it overrun with Jerry plumbers.

MYSTERIOUS STRANGER: I am niet Jerry – ich bin Erich!

SCRATCHY: Stop it! This is getting us all nowhere. Sit down, Erich. Take the weight off your lederhosen. Enjoy your tea.

COLONEL: What? He's here to do a job of work.

SCRATCHY: Yes, well, I've got something to say about that.

VERONICA: Well?

SCRATCHY: You see, the boiler doesn't actually need mending at all. (pause) It just needs a match put to the pilot light.

LULU: Do you mean to say, we've been shivering here all this time and – all the time you've been – all the time….

SCRATCHY: Sorry, Lulu. It was all a sham. I just used it as an excuse to spend time down there searching for the Colonel's treasure.

WALTER: Ah, the treasure.

LULU: What?

VERONICA: (*trying to sound innocent*) What treasure?!
TARQUIN:

The COLONEL *splutters and twitches*

SCRATCHY: Well, I never did find it, Colonel. It's no good keeping up the pretence. We'll all freeze to death.

WPC. HASTINGS: (*searching for her notebook again*) Perhaps it's about time we had that chat, Colonel.

COLONEL: What? Of course not. What nonsense. Never heard such rot. The man's raving. He'll still be high on all those drugs they gave him at

	the hospital. (*to Thaargist*) You, get yourself up to the Manor. If there's nothing for you to do here, you can at least be fixing <u>my</u> boiler.
JEAN:	But Colonel, look outside. It's a blizzard now. I don't think anybody will be leaving here tonight. (*she moves to the French doors and wrenches them open*)
SOUND/LIGHTING FX/FX:	SNOW BLOWS IN VIOLENTLY, WIND HOWLING LOUDLY. *Opening the door causes the electrics to falter again. The* OUTSIDE LIGHT COMES ON WITH A SPLUTTER. JEAN *closes the door with some difficulty, but the electrics are still playing up.* ALL THE LIGHTS FLICKER *and the* RADIOGRAM *throws out static.*
LULU:	Careful, Jean.
COLONEL:	Blizzard or no, this Kraut is going to get my boiler working whether he likes it or not (*he raises the gun and points it the* MYSTERIOUS STRANGER*)* Come on you, get your tools and move yourself.

MYSTERIOUS STRANGER: Mien tools are in ze van. I hef nuzzing on me but zis rusty knife. (*he produces a knife from his back pocket*)

COLONEL: Watch out! He's got a weapon! (*he takes a step towards the MYSTERIOUS STRANGER who takes a step backwards in alarm.*)

SOUND/LIGHTING FX: The LIGHTS FLICKER BRIEFLY. The OUTSIDE LIGHT FLICKERS AND BUZZES LOUDLY as the WIND HOWLS.

JEAN: What's going on?

LIGHTING FX: BLACKOUT

Screams from VERONICA and LULU. There is a general hub-ub and confusion.

WALTER: Where's the candles?

TARQUIN: Who's that?

PC. HASTINGS: (*almost together*) Everybody stay still!

SCRATCHY: Get off my leg!

SOUND FX: A CAT SCREECHES

FX: The COLONEL's gun goes off.

SOUND/LIGHTING FX: The OUTSIDE LIGHT FLICKERS AND BUZZES *and in that light, we see the* MYSTERIOUS STRANGER *making a hasty exit through the French doors.* WIND HOWLS *and more* SNOW BLOWS IN. *After another very brief* BLACKOUT, ALL THE LIGHTS COME BACK UP. *The* COLONEL *is sprawled across the table, his head hidden over the upstage side of the table.*

LULU *screams and points at the* COLONEL.

SOUND FX: RADIOGRAM *sparks into life as the* CURTAIN FALLS *quickly.*

RADIO:(*carol*) In the bleak mid-winter
Frosty wind made moan,
Earth stood hard as iron,
Water like a stone.
Snow had fallen, snow on snow,
Snow on snow....   (*fade*)

END OF ACT TWO

Act Three: Scene One

SOUND FX: *The* RADIOGRAM *plays* Zambezi *by Lou Busch. Sound of birdsong from garden which continues occasionally and faintly in the background until Veronica's entrance on page 44.*

The CURTAIN RISES. *It is about 6 months later, a bright afternoon in the summer of 1964 (Saturday 4th July 1964). The clock shows 2:55.*

The French doors are wide open, and we can see that the 'CatRy' sign and cat pen have been removed and replaced with an ornamental bush in a large pot and a fresh backdrop with a view of a well-tended garden. The defective outside light has been replaced with a new one. The set has been completely 'redecorated'. The top half of the walls are now freshly painted, and a dado rail has been added with 1960s style, jazzy wallpaper below. In the kitchen area a tiled splashback has been installed in vibrant colours, the gingham curtains below the work surface have been removed, as has the ancient dresser and new fitted cupboards and shelves are in their place. The old pine kitchen table and chairs have been replaced with a smaller, Habitat style table and 2 chairs in gleaming stainless steel and glass, which sit against the wall R, upstage from the cellar door. A vase of flowers, a fruit bowl and a lamp with a metal stand and a contemporary shade are on the table. The old black telephone has been replaced by a 'modern', push-button one in a gentle pastel shade. About the only thing that has not changed is the radiogram which is playing Zambezi by Lou Busch.

SCRATCHY *enters UC from the garden. He is dressed more elegantly than before, even though he is dressed for gardening. He has new glasses and wears a green, padded, sleeveless gilet and trilby (his gardening hat). The trouser leg of his wooden leg is still in tatters, as though this is a part of his persona that he will never lose. He goes to the radiogram and changes the station. He takes off his hat and puts it on the table, removes his gilet, which he hangs at the bottom of the stairs and then carefully chooses an apple from the fruit bowl. He then exits DR into the cellar, biting into the apple.*

SOUND FX:	RADIOGRAM *crackles and settles on a gardening program.*
SOUND FX:	**RADIO ANNOUNCER:** So, Percy, it's that time of year when people are hoping they can sit back and enjoy the rewards of all their hard work earlier in the year. Is it time to get the deckchairs out? (SCRATCHY *snorts at this before selecting an apple and exiting into the cellar*)
SOUND FX:	**PERCY THROWER:** Oh, no, no, no, no, no, no. There's never a time when a dedicated gardener shouldn't be out in his garden with

	at least a fork in his hand. (LULU *enters UR through the arch*) At this time of year the weeds can be a real problem. Why....... (LULU *flicks the switch on the* RADIOGRAM *and it instantly changes to* I Want to Hold Your Hand *by The Beatles.*)
LULU:	That's better. (*she dances the Frug for a few seconds before she exits through the French doors and goes out R*) Walter!

JEAN *enters from UL and through the French doors immediately. She sees that there is no-one there and goes to the* RADIOGRAM *and changes the station. She is carrying a small ornamental white china cat which she adds to a row of ornamental cats on a shelf in the kitchen area, adjusting them all to her satisfaction. She moves to the table and tidies it, taking great care over the positioning of the lamp.*

SOUND FX:	RADIOGRAM *crackles and whistles and fades into a tennis commentary. We hear a tennis ball being hit.*
SOUND FX:	**DAN MASKELL:** Oh, I say, that's a magnificent return down the line by Maria Bueno. (*Umpire calls in the background* "Game to Miss Bueno. Miss Bueno leads by four games to

two in the final set.") What a little powerhouse she is. Margaret Court has done well to fight back after that one loss of serve in the first set and to force Maria Bueno into a three setter but now it seems the little dynamo from Brazil can do no wrong. The players have changed ends and now it's Bueno to serve. (*sound of a tennis ball being hit into the net.*)

UMPIRE: Net, second service. (*sound of another tennis ball being hit*)

DAN MASKELL: The second serve is deep, and Margaret returns across court, but Maria Bueno is on it in a flash. Margaret tries to lob in reply but it's – out!

(JEAN *shrugs, picks up* SCRATCHY's *hat, which she strokes affectionately, and exits DL [we presume to hang it up in the hall]*)

UMPIRE: Out. Fifteen Love.

DAN MASKELL: I must say I've not seen such cracking tennis since the last time these two played

in the finals of the French Open
earlier this year.

WALTER *enters at this point and the following line is heard over his and* LULU's *entrance.*

WALTER *enters UC at the French doors, prancing in, almost ballet-dancer like from the R. He is dressed in tennis whites, with his shorts down to his knees and two skinny legs sticking out the bottom rather pathetically. He no longer wears his thick-lensed glasses, and he sports a gaily coloured, spotted neckerchief and a white headband. He stops in the door with his tennis racquet held coquettishly over his shoulder and his knees bent as if serving (girlishly). At the same moment* SCRATCHY *enters DR and* JEAN *enters DL.*

WALTER:	Anyone for tennis? (SCRATCHY *and* JEAN *are aghast and stand transfixed*)
DAN MASKEL	- but this time it seems the play is in Miss Bueno's favour. Is it those frilly knickers? Who knows?
LULU:	(*enters UC and stops next to* WALTER *in the doorway*) Oh, there you are, you silly boy. What on earth are you doing?
SOUND FX:	LULU *moves to the* RADIOGRAM *and turns it off.*

WALTER: Well, now I do feel like an idiot.

SCRATCHY: That's good, because that's exactly how you look.

LULU *moves back to* WALTER *and kisses him on the lips.*

LULU: Oh, I do love you, Walter. You're the first boyfriend I've ever had who really makes me laugh.

WALTER: (*lowering his racquet*) Oh, I say. Do I really?

LULU *and* WALTER *stand staring into one another's eyes.*

JEAN: (*dreamily, looking at Scratchy*) Oh, to be so young - and so in love.

LULU *links her arm through* WALTER's *and leads him out into the garden. They exit UR.*

SCRATCHY: If the boy makes my girl happy what more can a father ask? Even if he does look like a tit in a trance.

JEAN: The sun is shining; the birds are singing, and all is well with the world. Who would have thought any of this would be possible last Christmas, eh? With the Colonel slumped over the table, dead as a

	dodo – and us all thinking he was the one who killed Mavis.
SCRATCHY:	Now, now, Jean. The coroner said it was an accident - death by misadventure – so, please, don't go opening up old wounds again with your wild theories.

JEAN *fiddles with her pearl necklace and ponders a moment, before smiling, slapping* SCRATCHY *hard across the back causing Scratchy to totter.*

JEAN:	Bravo that man! That's the spirit, best not dwell on the past.
SCRATCHY:	We've a lot to be thankful for. Lulu and I could have been turned out on our ear, but Tarquin and Veronica have been very kind, letting us stay on.
JEAN:	Don't be so gullible, Scratchy. Who's done all the work round here? You've taken down the old cattery, you've transformed that garden - and look at all the work you've done in here. You've rewired the place, boarded over the well again, redecorated the whole

house. And all because Mrs Hoity-Toity smartie-pants asked you to.

LULU and WALTER enter through French doors. LULU is carrying a small bunch of flowers that she has picked from the garden. She hands these to WALTER so that she can open an envelope that she is also carrying, out of which she extracts a 45rpm record in its sleeve.

SCRATCHY: I couldn't have done it without you, Jean. You've been a rock. And Lulu's time at Art School has helped. She picked out all the décor and the new furniture. And Veronica and Tarquin have paid for it all.

In the background, LULU and WALTER are whispering to each other romantically. LULU bends towards WALTER to kiss him again. One leg bends up at the knee. This is followed by one of WALTER's legs bending up at the knee. JEAN bends towards Scratchy and kisses him on the cheek. One leg bends up at the knee.

JEAN: You're a sweet, sweet man, Scratchy, but you're very naïve. Tarquin and Veronica don't do anything without an ulterior motive. You mark my words, there's something in the air. We just don't know what it is yet.

SCRATCHY: Well, I'm taking one day at a time, Jean. I don't have your naturally suspicious mind. I'd rather think the best of people until they give me reason not to.

VERONICA: (*off R*) Come on, come on, you two. It can't be that heavy.

SOUND FX: BIRDSONG STOPS

LULU: (*breaking away from her clinch with WALTER*) Oh God, it's that awful woman again.

WALTER: Do you mean my mother?

LULU: Oh, I'm sorry, Walter, but she's so – so...

WALTER: Don't say it.

LULU: Come on, let's go upstairs and put some records on. Hey - I've got a new Dansett! (*waving a 45rpm record in her hand*) We can listen to 'A Hard Day's Night'.

WALTER: What's that?

LULU: The Beatles! it hasn't even been released over here yet. A friend of

	mine sent me a copy from the States. It's hot!!
WALTER: (*totally mesmerised by Lulu*)	What's a Dansett?
LULU: (*laughing*)	Walter you say the funniest things! Come on, I'll teach you how to Frug. (*she exits UR up the stairs making 'Frug' dance moves. WALTER shrugs at SCRATCHY and JEAN and then follows LULU trying (badly) to imitate her moves.*) (*off*) And then there's the Monkey and the Dog. We'll get that heart pumping!
JEAN:	Have you any idea what they're talking about?
SCRATCHY:	I hope not.

VERONICA *appears at the open French doors, entering from the R. She stops and stands with her hands on hips, staring back the way she has come, looking impatient. She is elegantly dressed in a wide-brimmed floppy summer hat and a floaty dress.*

VERONICA:	What are you two doing?
TARQUIN: (*off*)	It's bloomin' heavy.
VERONICA:	I've never known such a pair of little wimps. Put your backs into it. (*she

enters and moves DC. To SCRATCHY, *noticeably ignoring* JEAN) Ah, there you are, Jack. I have a little job for you.

JEAN: Another one?

VERONICA: (*ignoring Jean*) It won't take you a moment.

JEAN: Nothing ever does when someone else does it for you.

TARQUIN *and* HASTINGS *appear at the French doors, entering from the R. They are struggling to carry a large metal sign, about 3-4 feet wide by 15" high, which we can only see the back of.* TARQUIN *drops his end to the ground and leans heavily on the sign.*

WPC. HASTINGS: (*out of breath*) Where do you want it, Mrs Pigeon?

VERONICA: How many times must I tell you? It's Mrs Bulstrode Pyke now – and it has been for nearly three months. Can you get nothing right? Why don't you write it down in your little police notebook thingy.

WPC. HASTINGS: Sorry Mrs Pigeon. (*gasps for breath*) Where do you want it Mrs Bulstrode Pyke?

VERONICA: (*snapping her fingers*) Bring it here.
(HASTINGS' *shoulders drop.*
TARQUIN *glares at her but doesn't move*) Come on, chop, chop.

Slowly and begrudgingly the two men raise up the sign again, struggling under the weight.

JEAN: She sounds just like the Colonel. All she needs is a twelve-bore shotgun and a moustache and you'd just never tell the difference.

SCRATCHY: She wears the dress better though.

VERONICA: Very funny, Jack. (*to Tarquin*) Are you coming?

JEAN: (*to Scratchy*) Jack?

SCRATCHY: She can't bring herself to call me Scratchy. She says it sounds common.

TARQUIN: (*to* HASTINGS *as the start to enter through French doors*) I'll swear she's trying to kill us.

VERONICA: (*indicating DC and stepping out of the way DL*) Just here.

TARQUIN *and* HASTINGS *struggle indoors with the sign.* TARQUIN *starts to put his end down again.*

VERONICA: Don't put it down! Not on the new rug. That cost me a fortune. Well, turn it round. (*There is a little business while* TARQUIN *and* HASTINGS *can't agree (silently) which way round they are going. The sign is visible but upside-down*) Other way up. (*More business while* TARQUIN *and* HASTINGS *engineer the heavy sign to go the right way up without it touching the floor. We now see that the sign says* 'PAMPERED PUSSIES' *with a suitable cat-style logo at each end*)

JEAN: What on earth is that?

VERONICA: My new venture. (*there is a pregnant pause while no-one knows what to say*) I'm opening a Pussy Parlour.

JEAN: A what?!

SCRATCHY: Don't ask.

VERONICA: A pussy parlour, dear. They're all the rage in London now. People will flock here to have their pussies groomed, get their nails clipped, a quick shampoo and blow dry. I intend to attract a better class of clientele. The right people want their pussies pampered these days. And it will be so much better than that horrid cattery. No smelly pens, no feeding, no cleaning up after them. The punters just drop off their cats for an hour or two, we pamper them and hand them back.

JEAN: Well, I've never had my pussy pampered and I'm not about to start now.

SCRATCHY: And where are you going to do that? In the village High Street? I'm sorry, Mrs Bulstrode Pyke, but I can't quite see you up to your arms in soap suds and nail clippers.

VERONICA: Well, of course you can't – and I won't be. It's going to be here – and don't expect me to be handling no cats myself. Good gracious, who do you think I am? They have teeth and claws you know. No, no, you and Louisa shall be running it.

SCRATCHY: But - ?

JEAN: Where?

VERONICA: Here, of course. I didn't lug this sign all the way down here for my health. (TARQUIN *coughs*. HASTINGS *just looks on open-mouthed*) Well, you know what I mean.

JEAN: (*to* SCRATCHY) What did I tell you? This is what she's wanted all along.

VERONICA: I'm sorry, but I can't believe you expected to live here rent free forever and not pay your way. No, if you want to stay on here then I must insist that you and Louisa look after this little business for me. Walter will handle all the paperwork – when I tell him to. And Tarquin will – well he'll do something I suppose.

JEAN: And what will you be doing?

VERONICA: Supervising of course. Someone has to be in charge, and I will still be seen in the London Spotlight. I <u>am</u> still an actress, you know. I cannot neglect my public forever. Now then, let's start by getting this sign up. Jack, fetch a ladder. Tarquin, Hastings, I want this up on the wall just outside here, above the door. People will be able to see it from the road. (*everyone looks at each other*) Come on, come on, get a move on!

SOUND FX: HASTINGS *stops to wipe his brow, cocks an ear upwards to SOUNDS OF MUSIC (Hard Day's Night by The Beatles)* WALTER *and* LULU *laughing.* HASTINGS *becomes visibly jealous.*

WPC. HASTINGS: Is that your son upstairs?

VERONICA: (*couldn't care less*) Probably.

VERONICA *stands admiring the sign which* TARQUIN *struggles to take the weight of as* HASTINGS *lets go of it, dropping her end.*

TARQUIN: Hell's bells girl! You nearly had my foot off!

WPC. HASTINGS: Is he up there with Miss Louisa?

SCRATCHY: Yes, with my full consent.

LULU: (*off*) No, Walter, put that there...oh, show a bit of enthusiasm, you'll like it when you get the hang of it. (*giggling*) I'll have to get my last boyfriend back, 'Fingers'. He could show you a thing or two. Now watch what you're doing with your elbows.

WPC. HASTINGS: (*crossing to the bottom of stairs, she is seething*) What the - !?

WALTER: (*off*) Sorry. I guess I'm just not good at this sort of thing.

HASTINGS *moves back to* TARQUIN *and* VERONICA *as if pleading for their help.*

LULU: (*off*) Look, that bit goes there...that's it, (*giggling*) now isn't that better? Do this right and I'll show you my Monkey, and then we can have a go at the Dog. And if you're a very good boy I'll let you see my Mashed Potato!

WPC. HASTINGS: (a*lmost screaming, running up 2 or 3 stairs*) What are they doing up there?!

JEAN: Frugging.

WPC. HASTINGS: (*rushing towards Scratchy*) I'll arrest him!

VERONICA: Arrest my boy - on what charge?

WPC. HASTINGS: (*flailing her arms wildly, mad with jealousy and rage*) A breach of the peace!

SCRATCHY: The only one who's causing a commotion is you.

JEAN: Well said, that man. Now shut up, Constable...

VERONICA: For once we are in agreement, Now, get hold of this sign and we can get my business up and running.

Reluctantly HASTINGS does as she is told all the while scowling toward the direction of upstairs.

TARQUIN: (*angry under his breath*) Outside with it, again then!

TARQUIN and HASTINGS carry the sign back outside and continue for a while to manoeuvre it into the right position.

SOUND FX: MUSIC STOPS

VERONICA: The ladder, Jack, if you please!

SCRATCHY: (*tugs forelock sarcastically*) I'll do it directly, Mrs Bulstrode Pyke.

SCRATCHY *exits DR into cellar.*

JEAN: (*agitated*) You've got them all chasing around after you, haven't you? That's your <u>real</u> business, isn't it? Not being an actress or running a Pussy Parlour. You just want to be the centre of attention – and you don't care who you have to tread on while you're doing it.

VERONICA: Are you talking to me? If so, you can alter that tone of voice. <u>I</u> am the Lady of the Manor now and don't you forget it.

JEAN: That's hardly likely. (*Looking Veronica up and down*) You've done very well for yourself, haven't you? Quite the rags to riches story. How convenient this has all been for you. You appear out of the blue and the next thing we know, Mavis dies, and then the Colonel. Before you know it, there you are, Queen of all you survey. Lady of the Manor, budding entrepreneur. What next? Or should I say, who next? Tarquin perhaps? He's served his purpose...

VERONICA: Are you accusing me of...how dare you, you frustrated old hag!

SOUND FX: DOORBELL RINGS

JEAN: I say it as I see it, Veronica. If I were Tarquin, I'd watch my back.

VERONICA: (*threateningly*) If I really were a murderer, as you seem to be implying, you might have just signed your own death warrant, Jean Palmer.

SOUND FX: DOORBELL RINGS

TARQUIN: Someone is at the door, V!

VERONICA: (*obstinate*) I'm not deaf.

JEAN: (*sarcastically, making a mock curtsy*) Why don't I go, your ladyship?

JEAN *exits huffily DL.* VERONICA, *feeling that she got the better of the exchange, soaks up her feeling of superiority, runs a finger across tabletop and moves the table a few inches downstage, lining it up carefully to be exactly central below a picture hanging on the wall. She carefully adjusts the lamp and smiles a satisfied smile.* JEAN *re-enters DL with* MYSTERIOUS STRANGER, *this time in guise of* LADY HATTIE CHRISAGA, *a well-dressed, if rather Edwardian looking lady for the swinging sixties. 'She' is an elderly woman in an ankle length, sombre dress and broad-brimmed feathered hat. Her heels are too high for a lady of her age, so she teeters dangerously. She wears a pair of lorgnettes on a ribbon around her neck, has a constant shake and carries a wicker cat basket in one hand and a silver topped cane in the other (the same one that was used by Archie Gathasit).*

MYSTERIOUS STRANGER: I happened to be passing and saw your workmen with the sign out front and I thought 'Hattie, my dear, that is just what you require, your pussy hasn't been pampered in years'.

VERONICA: (*under her breath*) Oh, for God's sake, this peasant stock... (*loudly, assuming the old lady is deaf*) We are not open yet!

MYSTERIOUS STRANGER: There's no need to shout. (*to JEAN*) Why is she shouting? I am not accustomed to being spoken to in that fashion. I am Lady Hattie Chrisaga, and these are my cats, Tommy and Tuppence. (*places basket on floor*)

VERONICA: (*total transformation*) Did you say 'Lady'? Please come in, take a seat.

TARQUIN: How high do you want this bally sign, V?

WPC. HASTINGS: (*puffing*) I could tell her where to put it.

MYSTERIOUS STRANGER *looks disapprovingly at the 'workmen' using her lorgnette. Embarrassed*, VERONICA *laughs like a horse which then causes increased disapproval from* MYSTERIOUS STRANGER. JEAN *savours* VERONICA's *discomfort.*

VERONICA: (*to* TARQUIN)   Not now, darling, duty calls.

SCRATCHY *emerges from cellar covered in dust with an old wooden 'A' frame ladder which is filthy. He props it noisily against wall.*

MYSTERIOUS STRANGER: And what have we here; another troglodyte?

VERONICA: Take that ladder outside, this instant, Jack. How dare you come through the parlour with it. (*to* MYSTERIOUS STRANGER)   So difficult to find decent staff since the war. I'm sure you have the same problem.

SCRATCHY: (*does as instructed but mutters*) Women! How else am I to get from A to B - fly?

SCRATCHY *erects the steps outside the French windows which* HASTINGS *goes up and they start erecting the sign.* TARQUIN *stands by ineffectually. The* MYSTERIOUS STRANGER *beckons*

JEAN *with her cane and uses it to point at the cat basket* JEAN *shrugs, shakes her head, pondering what to do with it.*

VERONICA: Lemon tea, Lady Chris...

MYSTERIOUS STRANGER: ...aga, Chrisaga of the famous Cotswold Chrisaga's. Our estate spans over half the golden-honeycombed picture-postcard land of the Cotswold's. Everything hoofed bears our brand, every tenant farmer pays their homage and thanks their lucky stars they plough and sow for us; do I make myself clear? (*she shakes her cane at Jean and the basket again*)

VERONICA: But of course, how remiss of me. Jean please would you take Tommy and Tuppence next door and – look after them?

JEAN: Me?

VERONICA: Yes.

JEAN: Next door?

VERONICA: Next door. (*meaningfully*) Where we look after the cats. (*she picks up the basket and thrusts it into JEAN's hands, then shushes her out of the*

French doors backwards saying...) Tommy and Tuppence deserve the very best attention. Give them the whole works, shampoo and set, blow-dry, clawdicure. I'm sure you know what you're doing. (*VERONICA grabs TARQUIN by the collar and yanks him inside while pushing JEAN out with the other hand. She shuts the French doors firmly on JEAN who is left floundering open-mouthed at the door for a few moments before she takes the cats off UL*) (*turning quickly and trying to hide JEAN, to MYSTERIOUS STRANGER*) Lemon tea, Lady Chrisaga?

MYSTERIOUS STRANGER: I never take tea after 3:00 in the afternoon.

VERONICA: Where have I heard that before? (*moves C*) Are you sure we haven't met?

MYSTERIOUS STRANGER: (*aghast at the very thought*) You and I? Mixing in the same social circles? I hardly think that likely. (*to TARQUIN*) Young man, don't you have some work that you should be getting on with?

TARQUIN: (*extending a hand which he wipes on his trousers*) Tarquin Bulstrode Pyke, at your service. Together with my good lady wife, we are the owners of this establishment. Such a privilege to meet you, Lady - I didn't catch the name?

MYSTERIOUS STRANGER: (*disdain*) That's because I did not throw it. Now do whatever it is you do with Tommy and Tuppence and send me the bill.

TARQUIN: Right oh. Where do we send it?

MYSTERIOUS STRANGER: Am I dealing with amateurs?

VERONICA: (*scolding*) Tarquin, really! Have no fear, Lady Chrisaga, we will sort this to your utmost satisfaction.

MYSTERIOUS STRANGER: I sincerely hope so. Now, I bid you a good day. (*she turns imperiously and heads for the door DL*)

VERONICA *watches the* MYSTERIOUS STRANGER *begin to exit DL, tottering in her high heels. They almost buckle under her.*

VERONICA: Just a minute. Harold? (MYSTERIOUS STRANGER *stops abruptly*) Is that you? I'd know that wiggle anywhere.

MYSTERIOUS STRANGER: (*turns slowly NOW USING OWN VOICE*) Gerald.

VERONICA: But you're –

MYSTERIOUS STRANGER: Gerald.

VERONICA: Dead.

MYSTERIOUS STRANGER: Not yet, Veronica.

VERONICA: (*rushing to embrace him*) Oh, Harold. I thought I'd never see you again!

MYSTERIOUS STRANGER: (*keeping her at arm's length*) I don't suppose you did. And it's Gerald. You never could get it right, could you.

TARQUIN: You know each other?

MYSTERIOUS STRANGER: So, this is number four. (*to Tarquin*) I hope she at least remembers your name. I was number two, Gerald Edgware. I would like to say I am pleased to meet you, but I fear it might be a short acquaintance.

TARQUIN: I don't understand.

MYSTERIOUS STRANGER: I'm sure that's the quality she most admires in you.

VERONICA: I think you should leave.

MYSTERIOUS STRANGER: Oh no, not now that the cat's out of the bag, Veronica. I think Tarquin deserves to know what to expect.

TARQUIN: What are you talking about?

MYSTERIOUS STRANGER: This might come as something of a shock to you, Tarquin, but you're blushing bride blushed at least three times before you – and that's just the ones I know about. It doesn't include the ones that never made it as far as the altar, of course. They only count as minor diversions in Veronica's exotic history.

VERONICA: If you don't leave now, I shall call the police. In fact, there's one outside right now.

MYSTERIOUS STRANGER: That ridiculous lump? She couldn't detect her own face in a mirror. But call the police if you wish. They would be more than pleased to hear what I have to say.

You see, Tarquin, Veronica has been married many times.

TARQUIN: Are you a bigamist?!

MYSTERIOUS STRANGER: Nothing so sordid, Tarquin. What did the first one die of, Veronica? Over-exertion in the bedroom department, wasn't it?

VERONICA: A heart attack. He worked too hard.

MYSTERIOUS STRANGER: And you made sure he had a lot of bills to pay. And then there was number two – who mysteriously fell off a cliff and was lost at sea.

VERONICA: It was such a foggy night, Harold – Gerald. And you have no witnesses.

MYSTERIOUS STRANGER: Luckily, a passing mountain goat broke my fall, and I landed on a ledge with nothing worse than a twisted ankle and a bruised ego. It was, however, a most convenient way to get out of a loveless marriage and so I quietly disappeared. I did not take a great deal of interest in you again, Veronica, until I heard about the

	mysterious and unlikely death of Roger Pigeon, the well-known financier, who I understand had the good sense to leave all his worldly wealth to a cat's home in Norwich – much to your chagrin I would imagine.
VERONICA:	You can prove nothing.
MYSTERIOUS STRANGER:	(*to* TARQUIN) Take care, old man. Your days might be numbered.
TARQUIN:	Get out! You're a charlatan and a fraud. This is nothing but a blackmail ploy and we shan't be taken in. Get out, before I throw you out! (*the shouts attract the attention of* HASTINGS *and* SCRATCHY *outside who we see peering through the window.* SCRATCHY *is seen beckoning to* JEAN *who joins them a few moments later.*)
MYSTERIOUS STRANGER:	I'm leaving. I have been following you everywhere, Veronica, for the past two years, just waiting for you to make another mistake. Don't worry, I shall catch you out yet.

TARQUIN: Get out!

The MYSTERIOUS STRANGER *turns abruptly and totters towards the exit DL. He gets halfway before his ankles buckle again. He takes his shoes off and strides purposefully to the door, where he turns back to look at* TARQUIN)

MYSTERIOUS STRANGER: By the way. You ought to know that none of her previous marriages survived more than three months. *(he exits quickly)*

TARQUIN: How much of that was true?

VERONICA: He was making it all up.

TARQUIN: So, he didn't fall off a cliff?

VERONICA: No – I mean, yes. He fell off the cliff, but it <u>was</u> a very foggy night, and it <u>was</u> just an accident. (*pause*) And my first husband did die of a heart attack.

TARQUIN: Over-work?

VERONICA: I really don't want to talk about it.

TARQUIN: *(sternly)* I'm sure you don't. Try.

VERONICA: We were on honeymoon. At Bartram's Hotel in Corfu. He was somewhat older than I was, and the excitement rather got to him. I wasn't to know he had a weak heart.

TARQUIN: How much older?

VERONICA: I was 25. (*pause*) He was 75.

TARQUIN: 50 years?! And the second one you pushed over a cliff.

VERONICA: Tarquin!

SOUND FX: A Hard Day's Night *is heard coming from* LULU's *bedroom as the noise of the argument brings* WALTER *and* LULU *down from upstairs. They stop at the bottom step watching open-mouthed, but* TARQUIN *and* VERONICA *are too involved in their argument to notice them. The record upstairs has been set to replay so it continues throughout this scene but does not become really noticeable until* TARQUIN *is left alone on the stage.*

TARQUIN: And what about the third one?

VERONICA: I don't want to talk about it anymore.

TARQUIN: (*getting more and more worked up*) Obviously, or you would have told me before now. I'm not a complete fool, Veronica. Everyone has to have a past but being married is supposed to mean sharing things like that. I can't believe you've been married three times before and I knew nothing about it.

VERONICA: I didn't think it was important.

TARQUIN: Not important?! (*he twitches*) Two men lie dead, three as far as you knew, and it's not important! (*he twitches violently and his wig falls off. He valiantly tries to put it back on during the rest of the speech*) And what about Walter? Does he know about all of this? Which one was his father?

VERONICA: (*long pause*) None of them.

TARQUIN: (*twitches and the wig comes off again, followed by WALTER also twitching*) Damn! (*retrieves wig and vainly tries to get it back on*)

VERONICA: (*moves towards TARQUIN*) I'm not going to talk about this anymore until you have calmed down. You shall just have to learn to trust me, Timothy – Tarquin. (*she moves quickly to the French windows where* JEAN, HASTINGS *and* SCRATCHY *are straining to hear what is going on. She opens the doors and turns dramatically*) You don't know what that man is like, Tarquin. Things might not be quite as they seem! (*she exits quickly and slams the door behind her.*)

HASTINGS *and* JEAN *sidestep to left and right of the French windows but* SCRATCHY, *who is right in* VERONICA's *path as she exits UR, is left spinning in her wake directly under the new sign, which falls and hits him on the head.* SCRATCHY *falls to the floor in a heap.* JEAN *immediately kneels beside him and gently tries to bring him round*))

TARQUIN: And don't come back until you can start telling me the truth!

WALTER: Tarquin?

TARQUIN: Get out! Leave me alone! (*he slumps into the chair US of the table R*)

JEAN: (*beckons to* HASTINGS *to take overlooking after* SCRATCHY *and enters UC*) (*quietly*) Tarquin? Is everything alright?

TARQUIN: Of course it's not. Why can't you all leave me alone?! (*he puts his head in his hands*)

JEAN: (*to Lulu*) Get your father a glass of water, Lulu. (*fishes in her pocket and pulls out a key on a fob*) Walter, here's my car keys. When he comes round, get Scratchy to hospital. He's had a nasty bump to the head. (*hands* WALTER *the key*)

LULU *goes to the kitchen and pours a large glass of water.* WALTER *exits UC and he and* HASTINGS *try to prop up* SCRATCHY's *limp form. They loosen his collar and fan him.* JEAN *moves R and puts her hand on* TARQUIN's *shoulder.*

JEAN: Can I get you anything, Tarquin?

LULU: I'll get him some water too, shall I? Or how about a nice cup of tea?

JEAN: (*ignoring the snipe*) I think he's going to need something stronger. (LULU *exits UC with a glass of water which she tries to get* SCRATCHY *to sip. He is still out cold.*) Tarquin, I can't pretend to know what just went on here, but you and Veronica have obviously had a bit of a spat.

TARQUIN: Brilliant.

JEAN: Why don't you go after her and try to patch things up.

TARQUIN: It's too late for that.

LULU: (*calling to Jean*) He won't drink it. I can't wake him up.

Irritated, JEAN *moves UC, takes the glass from* LULU's *hand and throws the water in* SCRATCHY's *face. He comes round instantly.)*

SCRATCHY: What the….?!

JEAN: Now get him off to the hospital all of you, and don't come back 'til he's all patched up.

JEAN *moves back to the table while* HASTINGS, WALTER *and* LULU *gather up a very groggy* SCRATCHY *and half carry him off R.*

JEAN: It's never too late, Tarquin. I really think you should go after her.

TARQUIN: And I think you should mind your own business.

JEAN: (*pauses but decides to let it ride. She turns and heads towards the door DL*) I'll get you a drink. (*she exits DL*)

TARQUIN: (*appearing to notice the music coming from upstairs for the first time*) Oh, shut up! Bloody racket! (*he goes to the bottom of the stairs and shouts up*) Will you turn that music off?!

JEAN: (*entering DL with a large brandy in a brandy glass and a magazine under her arm*) There's no-one up there. They've all gone off to the hospital with Scratchy.

TARQUIN: Oh, I hadn't noticed.

JEAN: No. You were a bit too busy feeling sorry for yourself. (*she leads him back to the table and sits him down*) Come and sit down. I've brought you a restorative and a magazine to read to take your mind off things. You just need to calm down and then I'm sure everything will sort itself out. (*she puts the glass in his hand, opens up the magazine and the places it on the table in front of* *him, smoothing out the pages for him*) Now you relax, and I'll go and turn the music off for you. (*she exits UR*)

TARQUIN *takes a gulp of brandy and coughs as though he is unused to strong drink. He looks quizzically at the glass and sniffs the drink. He shrugs and takes another sip as he picks up the magazine, which he peers at closely. He pats his pockets as though looking for a pair of glasses but can't find them. He puts the glass down and casually reaches to turn on the lamp...He pauses and sniffs the air. As he does so* VERONICA *appears at the French doors.*

VERONICA: (*acquiescently*)   Tarquin...

TARQUIN: Marmite, I can smell Marmite, I hate Marmite.

FX/SOUND FX: *The* LAMP BULB EXPLODES *as* TARQUIN *turns it on. The* MUSIC STOPS *instantly and there is the sound of a* HIGH ELECTRIC CURRENT.

VERONICA: Tarquin?   Tarquin!

TARQUIN *instantly goes rigid and then shakes through his whole body (his head twitching violently) as he is being electrocuted.* VERONICA *screams long and loud.*

LIGHTING FX: TOTAL BLACKOUT

END OF ACT THREE: SCENE ONE

Act Three: Scene Two

It is the morning of the next day. The break between these two scenes is only long enough for the actors to take up their new positions in the blackout and for the clock to be changed to about 10:30. During the blackout, which should be as near to total blackout as possible, TARQUIN *leaves the stage UR (In larger theatres, the safety curtain could be dropped at this point.).* LULU *sits where Tarquin had been.* WALTER *stands behind her and* SCRATCHY *is seated in the downstage chair. His head is swathed in a large bandage that comes down over one eye.* JEAN *is standing in the kitchen area drying some cups, which she puts away in a cupboard, and* HASTINGS *is DL. They are all turned towards* VERONICA, *who is standing in exactly the same place at the open French doors where she was at the end of Act Three: Scene One. Where possible, costume changes have taken place to indicate the passage of time – even if it is just the addition or removal of cardigans, jackets etc.* HASTINGS *is in full police uniform, including cap, and is holding her notebook with her pencil poised.* JEAN *is still wearing her habitual tweeds and pearls.*

In BLACKOUT *or as the curtain rises,* VERONICA *screams long and loud – an identical scream to the one at the end of the previous scene.*

LIGHTING FX: *The* LIGHTS COME UP

VERONICA: And then I fainted. (*She holds the back of her hand to her forehead* *and swoons gracefully to the floor a la Fay Wray in King Kong.* JEAN *provides a slow hand clap and* VERONICA *stands*)

WPC. HASTINGS: Yes, very dramatic, but we are here to give statements of the events that led to his death, not a full-blown re-enactment with sound effects.

JEAN: She's an actress, Hastings, she can't help it. Making a drama out of every little thing is her stock in trade.

VERONICA: Every little thing! My husband has just died! (*she produces a handkerchief from her sleeve and sniffs into it unconvincingly*)

WPC. HASTINGS: What I wanted to know, Mrs Pigeon, (VERONICA *glares at him*) – Mrs Bulstrode Pyke – is your movements up to the moment that you found the body.

JEAN: Yes, we all want to know that. What did you do after you left here - after your violent argument with your

WPC. HASTINGS: husband – and before you came back?

WPC. HASTINGS: If you don't mind, Miss Palmer, I shall ask the questions. My Sargent has given me strict instructions to take statements from you all and you will all get the chance to speak (*meaningfully to* JEAN) in due course. We even have the top brass coming down from Scotland Yard. They're sending their very best man to unravel... (*pondering*) ...now how did they put it? - ah yes, "this mysterious chain of death".

JEAN: (*smiling*) Really, they said that? Oh, how simply marvellous, it makes it sound just like an Agatha Christie novel.

LULU: Oh, Auntie Jean, how could you?

JEAN: (*picturing the title of a novel*) "Catastrophe in Devon". No – that's too obvious. How about "A Cat-alogue of Murder"? Yes, that would be it. (*They all stare at* JEAN *until* HASTINGS *breaks the silence.*)

Unnoticed by them all the MYSTERIOUS STRANGER, *in the guise of New York Detective,* INSPECTOR PETER COLHOURI, *enters at the French doors and leans nonchalantly on the doorframe.* COLHOURI *is dressed like Phillip Marlowe in trench coat and trilby. He has an unlit cigarette in one corner of his mouth.*

WPC. HASTINGS: (*refers to her notebook - to* VERONICA) What did you do after you left here - Mrs Bulstrode Pyke - and before you came back?

VERONICA: I'm not answering any of your impertinent questions, you silly little girl, in your silly little hat.

MYSTERIOUS STRANGER: (*Bronx accent*) Then perhaps the dame will talk to me.

All turn surprised. COLHOURI *moves through them, causing them to part like the Red Sea, they appear mesmerised by this man.*

SCRATCHY: Who the devil are you?

MYSTERIOUS STRANGER: (*smug*) Colhouri's the name, Peter Colhouri. (*he flashes a badge at them, showing it round too quickly for anyone to authenticate.* WALTER *almost falls over trying to follow the badge with his eyes as it glides past him*) Detective Inspector Peter Colhouri, 34th Precinct NYPD...

(*doffs brim of his hat*) ...at your service.

SCRATCHY: You don't look or sound like a proper detective to me.

MYSTERIOUS STRANGER: Says the guy who looks like he failed the audition for the Invisible Man.

WPC. HASTINGS: Oh, you'll be the bod' they've sent down from Scotland Yard.

MYSTERIOUS STRANGER: Give the guy a medal. (*sarcastically*) Or maybe I was just in the neighbourhood and popped in.

SCRATCHY: What is this? Some kind of exchange scheme?

WPC. HASTINGS: Oh yes, it's all the rage now. We had a French student last year.

LULU: (*thrilled*) I've never met a real American before. How thrilling.

MYSTERIOUS STRANGER: Hang in there sister, I'm a class act to follow.

WALTER: (*jealous*) I always find the Yank accent rather vulgar.

MYSTERIOUS STRANGER: (*to* LULU) Is Baby Face Nelson with you? No offence, but you could do better.

WALTER *puts up his fists as if to punch* COLHOURI *but restrains himself due to being a wimp.* LULU *puts her hand over one of* WALTER's *fists as if to restrain him, but all the while entranced by* COLHOURI. VERONICA *studies* COLHOURI *very closely, trying to peer under his hat and following him as he walks to and fro as though he were analysing the crime scene.*

JEAN: So, how can we be of assistance, Detective?

MYSTERIOUS STRANGER: (*to* HASTINGS) Bring me up to speed, will ya's.

WPC. HASTINGS: (*flustered, she fumbles through her notebook*) I was just about to...

COLHOURI *snatches* HASTINGS *notebook and throws it through the open French door.*

MYSTERIOUS STRANGER: (*prods a finger into* HASTINGS' *ample gut*) From here! Your gut feelings. Stow all that other crap, it's old school - history. A modern detective works on impulse, boom, boom, right to the heart of the crime... (*turns suddenly on*

VERONICA *who is still following him and observing too close for comfort*)
You got a problem, lady?!

VERONICA: (*smiling calmly*) No, not at all. I thought - no, never mind, you carry on. This is fascinating.

JEAN: But isn't it? Can I get anyone a drink?

MYSTERIOUS STRANGER: Bourbon - on the rocks.

LULU: (*swooning*) She means tea, I'm afraid.

MYSTERIOUS STRANGER: Nah! I ain't into that pansy stuff. Let's get on with this before the trail goes cold. Park your butts, people, this is gonna be a bumpy ride.

SCRATCHY *and* LULU *are already sitting in the only two available chairs. After a little shuffling of feet* LULU *gives up her seat to* JEAN *and stands behind that chair, hooking her arm through* WALTER's, *who looks suitably proud.* VERONICA *props herself against the frame of the French doors, places a cigarette in a holder languidly.* HASTINGS *shuffles up nearer to* COLHOURI *feeling that it's his duty to support him. From this point onwards,* HASTINGS *follows Colhouri's every move. She stands as close to him as possible, mimicking his hand movements, tipping her hat in unison etc.*

JEAN: So, where do we begin, Detective?

LULU: At the beginning, I suppose.

COLHOURI *paces like a shrewd cat after prey, he looks at each of them in turn, he clears his throat, they wait expectantly but he remains silent.*

WPC. HASTINGS: Would you rather I...

MYSTERIOUS STRANGER: Button it? Yeah.

WPC. HASTINGS: Yes – yes, of course, Sir.

SCRATCHY: Then what do we do?

VERONICA: (*lighting her cigarette as though bored by the whole proceedings*) I think he wants someone to confess.

MYSTERIOUS STRANGER: That would save us all a lot of time. Then I can get back over the pond and do some real work - with real New York hoods - none of this prissy, Limey, polite, drawing-room moider stuff.

JEAN: (*chuffed*) Finally, then you do believe we are dealing with moider - murder?!

MYSTERIOUS STRANGER: You seem like a wise old broad to me. What say <u>you</u> help me out here?

JEAN: (*delighted and flattered*) I don't mind if I do. I've always seen myself as a bit of a sleuth.

JEAN *stands, slapping her hands to her knees as she rises and bounds to join the detective.* HASTINGS *appears rather hurt by this apparent exclusion of his services.*

WPC. HASTINGS: Err, what about me?

MYSTERIOUS STRANGER: Sit down and shut up. Watch and learn buddy, watch, and learn, or go make these Limeys some tea.

Sulking, HASTINGS *sits in the chair vacated by* JEAN.

JEAN: (*excited*) Very well then. Murder number one, Mavis Hadley.

SCRATCHY: Steady on there, Jean!

MYSTERIOUS STRANGER: No, let her give it some vent. Hit me with what ya got.

WALTER *clenches a fist again which* LULU *pulls back down to his side rather too easily.*

JEAN: (*extracting paperwork from down her ample cleavage*) I took the liberty of making some notes.

HASTINGS *groans, head in hands.*

MYSTERIOUS STRANGER: Give the lady a break...the floor is yours.

JEAN: Thank you so much, Detective. Ooh, I've got goosebumps on my goosebumps. Right - ah yes, the first murder. (*stomps toward the cellar door*) It was here, or rather down there on the same night that poor President Kennedy was shot... (COLHOURI *makes the sign of the cross*) ...that my dearest friend and neighbour, Mavis Hadley, was so brutally slain...

MYSTERIOUS STRANGER: Brutally - how brutally? Was this a meat cleaver job? Brains splattered all over kitchen ceiling? Walls dripping with blood?

VERONICA: (*bored*) She tripped - and fell down the cellar stairs.

MYSTERIOUS STRANGER: Tripped? So, this Mavis woman was a junkie?

SCRATCHY: (*angry*) Hey, I won't have that thrown at my sister.

VERONICA: She tripped over her own feet.

MYSTERIOUS STRANGER: My apologies, I'm just trying to get up to speed here. (*to* JEAN) Go on, lady.

JEAN: Please, call me Jean. We were all down in the cellar because Scratchy had fallen down the well.

MYSTERIOUS STRANGER: Who or what is Scratchy? (SCRATCHY *raises his hand*) I see. And that's how come you've got the.... (*he waves his hand around his head to indicate the bandages*)

SCRATCHY: No.

JEAN: He broke his arm in two places, dislocated his shoulder and cracked three ribs. But that's another story. Don't get sidetracked.

MYSTERIOUS STRANGER: OK - enlighten me. So, you all go down the cellar to haul this guy's ass out of the well. Who was there?

JEAN: Lulu (LULU *smiles and waves at the detective*), Walter, myself...

MYSTERIOUS STRANGER: (*thoughtful, hand to chin*) Specific - give me the specific order people went down.

JEAN: (*impressed and slightly taken aback*) You've a keen brain, Detective Colhouri. I like that. Now let me see. Scratchy was obviously the first, then the Colonel, and then I think...

VERONICA: That's not true is it, Jean? <u>You</u> went down first after Scratchy's accident - and <u>before</u> the Colonel. You took the first aid kit down and came back looking like a refugee from the Blitz.

SCRATCHY: Is any of this important?

MYSTERIOUS STRANGER: If one of you's is the killer, yeah, it's pretty damned important! So again, from the top!

JEAN: Very well...Now let me see, there was me – and then…. well, I think it was….

WALTER: (*twitching*) Oh, for God's sakes! It was Miss Palmer, The Colonel, Tarquin (VERONICA *wipes a tear from here eye*) …sorry Mumsy. He went down at the same time as Constable Hasting's. Then I went down followed by my mother, then Jean again with Lulu, and that was the precise order.

WPC. HASTINGS: Spoken like a true accountant.

VERONICA: You beastly little woman.

MYSTERIOUS STRANGER: Quiet! Limey's, sheesh! So, that's the order. So now everyone's down in the cellar except the broad that died. Now who heard what? Especially from the deceased - any last words – strange noises?

SCRATCHY: This is in very poor taste.

JEAN, *unnoticed, steps into cellar DR, quietly opening and closing the door.*

VERONICA: (*staring hard at Lulu and overacting*) I heard her say quite clearly, "Get away from me, Lulu."

LULU: (*shocked*) Well, I heard Aunt Mavis say, "Turn the light on – (*pointedly*) Veronica."

WALTER: I don't like to argue with you my sweet, but what she actually said was...

JEAN: (*off*)　　　　"Hello, what are you doing there?"

LULU *stifles a scream, as does* WALTER *in quick succession.* JEAN *enters from cellar door DR.*

LULU:　　　　Yes – that was it.

MYSTERIOUS STRANGER:　　Do we concur? (*All reluctantly nod heads in various degrees of enthusiasm and agreement*) Let's get back to basics here. If we was downtown in the 34th Precinct I'd be takin' you's all down the slammer right now and treatin' ya to some rubber hose action. (WALTER *twitches and shudders*) They don't let me do that here, but we got to get some straight answers. Which of you guys wanted to see her dead?

SCRATCHY:　　Nobody. Don't be so ridiculous. The inquest said it was an accident. I don't believe she was murdered at all.

MYSTERIOUS STRANGER:　　If it was an accident, what the hell am I doing I doing here?

VERONICA:　　Good question.

MYSTERIOUS STRANGER: We'll get to you's later, lady. Who hated this woman enough to kill her? (*everyone turns slowly to look at LULU, who reacts with disbelief*)

LULU: Why is everyone looking at me? What was I going to inherit? Half a dozen cat bowls, and some broken down pens?

VERONICA: You hated her. I saw it from the minute I saw you together.

MYSTERIOUS STRANGER: How long you lived here? You'd know this place pretty well, I imagine. Every crook and nanny. I bet you could find yourself around this place with your eyes shut – even down in the cellar.

LULU: (*struggling to remember*) The last time I went down there was –

VERONICA: The night you killed Mavis?

LULU *bursts into tears.*

WALTER: Oh mother, look what you've done now. Do you have to be so cruel? (WALTER *puts his arm around* LULU)

VERONICA: She's a murderer, Walter. She doesn't deserve your sympathy. Come away from her.

WALTER: (*with venom*) I hate you. I wish you weren't my mother.

VERONICA: (*to* LULU) Do you see what you've done to my little boy?

SCRATCHY: (*to* VERONICA) And you leave my little girl alone. We were all quite happy here until you came along.

WPC. HASTINGS: (*indicating* WALTER) And him. I wouldn't trust him as far as I could throw him. He's a dark horse if you ask me.

WALTER: And what about you, Constable? What about Knuckles? As far as we know, you're the only one here who ever actually killed anyone.

MYSTERIOUS STRANGER: Knuckles?

LULU: (*weeping*) He was my first boyfriend. She killed him.

WPC. HASTINGS: Not that old one again. He topped himself while in police custody. I wasn't even on duty that night.

LULU: So you say.

MYSTERIOUS STRANGER: Nobody's asking you. I can see you're all like one big happy family. In fact, the only person who seems free from suspicion is - you, Mr Hadley.

SCRATCHY: What's that you say - me?

JEAN: It couldn't have been, Scratchy, he was down the well?

MYSTERIOUS STRANGER: It's a perfect alibi – always suspicious if you ask me. Okay, and the other two potential suspects just happen to be stiffs. How convenient for them.

VERONICA: One of those 'stiffs' was my husband.

JEAN: Move onto murder number two, Detective Colhouri, the Colonel.

MYSTERIOUS STRANGER: Right. Same routine people, where were you all and what were his last words.

VERONICA: He was fighting with the plum<u>b</u>er, Detective. Don't you remember?

MYSTERIOUS STRANGER: The plum<u>b</u>er?

LULU: Of course. The mysterious German plumber! What was his name?

WALTER: Thaargist – Erich Thaargist.

MYSTERIOUS STRANGER: You have an excellent memory, young man.

VERONICA: Better than yours.

WALTER: He had come to mend the boiler that wasn't broken, and he was waving a knife around.

MYSTERIOUS STRANGER: Slow down, young feller. If the boiler wasn't broke, why was he mending it? And where the does the knife come in? He stabbed the Colonel?

JEAN: The Colonel was shot.

MYSTERIOUS STRANGER: With a knife?

VERONICA: With a twelve-bore shotgun he just happened to have under his arm.

MYSTERIOUS STRANGER: The plumber?

JEAN: The Colonel.

MYSTERIOUS STRANGER: So, the Colonel shot himself because the plumber couldn't mend the boiler with his knife? You Brits slay me.

JEAN: I think this is going to take some time. I'll get us a bite to eat. (*she moves to the kitchen area and starts to get out plates, cups etc.*)

WALTER: Just a minute. We've forgotten someone. Archie Gathasit.

MYSTERIOUS STRANGER: Who he?

VERONICA: Oh, come now, Gerald, you must remember Archie Gathasit.

LULU: Gerald?

MYSTERIOUS STRANGER: (*to* VERONICA) Stow it!

LULU: I thought you said your name was Peter?

MYSTERIOUS STRANGER: Let's move on. This Colonel guy. Would he have any reason to kill Mavis?

SCRATCHY: Of course not.

JEAN: Oh yes.

MYSTERIOUS STRANGER: (*to* JEAN)   Explain.

JEAN: He'd been pestering her for months to get this house back from her. He would call in unannounced – ring her on the phone at all times of the day and night - he was making her life a misery.

LULU: But why?

SCRATCHY: The treasure. I started to tell you once before, but the Colonel's accident rather got in the way.

JEAN: You see, in the Civil War the Royalists had to hide their treasure from Oliver Cromwell.

WALTER: And the Colonel thought his ancestors hid their treasure in the cellar because there used to be a tunnel that led here from the Manor House. It's been blocked up and lost for years of course but….

SCRATCHY: How do you know all this?

WALTER: I've seen the papers – when I was cataloguing his library. I probably know more than he did. In fact, the most likely place was in the well

LULU: (*suspiciously*) How would you know that?

WALTER: I had a good look one day when you were all out – just before Scratchy came out of hospital. I found the loose brick marked with a crude 'C' below a crown – as described in one of his papers. I was hoping it might set us up for life, Lulu, but it wasn't to be.

SCRATCHY: What was meant to be in there?

WALTER: Two silver goblets, rubies, gold coins – oh, and a string of very valuable pearls. Apparently, it had one big pearl in the middle that was reputed to be the lost pearl of Charles the First. (JEAN's *hand goes to her string of pearls. Everyone looks at her quizzically*)

JEAN: Sorry – Woolworth's – 7/6d in the sale.

MYSTERIOUS STRANGER: (*to* WALTER) Did you tell anyone?

WALTER: Who me? What about?

MYSTERIOUS STRANGER: The treasure, of course.

WALTER: Well no. What with Mavis dying and then the Colonel – and there was no treasure anyway – it all seemed rather silly and pointless.

WPC. HASTINGS: Silly and pointless enough to kill two people for?

WALTER: How dare you?

WPC. HASTINGS: (*standing up and towering threateningly over* WALTER) I knew it was you all the time. I bet you knew about that treasure even before you came down here. I bet it was you who engineered getting Tarquin and Veronica together so that you could get down here and search for it. You killed Mavis and wheedled your way into poor Lulu's heart to have an excuse to keep visiting, and when the Colonel got this house back you killed him too.

WALTER: I've never heard such tosh. When the Colonel died it was Tarquin who inherited this house, not me.

WPC. HASTINGS: And now Tarquin's dead too.

VERONICA: Walter!

WALTER: Mumsy, don't listen to him. It's all in his imagination. If anyone killed all these people, it wasn't one of us. It was these mysterious strangers. Don't you see? As soon as a mysterious stranger appears, someone dies. Archie Gathasit, that actor fellow. He turns up looking for a room, quite out of the blue, and minutes later Mavis is dead. Has anybody heard or seen of him again? And the plumber, Erich Thaaargist, he arrives in a snowstorm without even a bag of tools and as quick as you can say 'Jack Robinson' the Colonel's dead – and the mysterious plumber disappears into the night, never to be seen again.

SCRATCHY: He's right you know. Yesterday it was that customer who turned up with her two cats. She left in a huff and, for some reason, Veronica and Tarquin had a blazing row and Tarquin ended up dead. (*Everyone turns to look at* VERONICA)

LULU: Who was she, Veronica?

VERONICA: You might well ask – mightn't she Gerald?

There is a pregnant pause while everyone turns to look at the MYSTERIOUS STRANGER *because* VERONICA *is staring hard at him.*

JEAN: (*moving to the table with a tray of cups and plates*) It seems that you are the mysterious stranger today, Detective Colhouri. Anyone for tea?

HASTINGS, WALTER *and* LULU *move towards the* MYSTERIOUS STRANGER threateningly. *The* MYSTERIOUS STRANGER *takes out a revolver and fires into air, they are all shocked, women scream and* WALTER *hides behind* LULU *then, bravely remembering he is a man steps in front of her but* LULU, *rather annoyed to be behind him tussles to regain front position in their relationship.*

MYSTERIOUS STRANGER: Right, let's have some calm here! Now my maths may not be that good but as far as I figure it, there were three murders. Mavis, the Colonel and then his son, Tarquin...

SCRATCHY *raise an arm for attention.*

MYSTERIOUS STRANGER: You wanna take a leak?

SCRATCHY: It's time to confess...oh no, not to the murders! But we're going to solve nothing today if someone doesn't start telling some truths. (*pause*) It's about Tarquin. (*pause*) He was my sister's son - by the Colonel...sorry Lulu, I always meant to tell you.

LULU: (*shocked*) You mean - we were related? – he was my.... ugh.

VERONICA: The dirty old dog. Alistair Bulstrode Pyke you certainly sowed your seed wide. Oh, what the hell, you may as well know, Walter, the Colonel was your father too.

WALTER: Oh, my god! (*to* LULU) Which means - <u>we're</u> sort of related!

WALTER *and* LULU *step slightly away from one another.* WALTER *takes out his handkerchief and cleans his togue on it.*

MYSTERIOUS STRANGER: (*nodding head*) Yeah, one big happy family. Any more? (to HASTINGS) Don't tell me – he was your Papa too.

WPC. HASTINGS: Don't be ridiculous. (*She twitches, exactly like the Colonel. Everyone stares at her*) What?!

MYSTERIOUS STRANGER: Let's not forget why we're here. The third stiff. Tarquin.

JEAN: He was electrocuted after an argument with Veronica.

SCRATCHY: (*bitter*) Like I said before, all of this started when <u>she</u> arrived.

VERONICA: I don't have to listen to another word of this!

MYSTERIOUS STRANGER: Just bear with me a while longer, we're almost done here. Tarquin was fried you say?

JEAN: Yes, in that chair where Scratchy is sitting. He'd reached out to turn the lamp on and...

MYSTERIOUS STRANGER: Fried. Let's take a look see.

MYSTERIOUS STRANGER *walks to study lamp and cable, closely observed by* HASTINGS.

WPC. HASTINGS: Seen anything to arouse suspicion, sir?

MYSTERIOUS STRANGER: The wires have been got at...and what's that smell?

VERONICA: Yes, the smell. Tarquin said he smelt Marmite just before he...

MYSTERIOUS STRANGER: ...fried.

JEAN: (*moving towards kitchen area*) Anyone hungry? (*no-one responds*)

VERONICA: Does this charade have to go on, Gerald?!

LULU: Why do you keep calling the detective, Gerald?

VERONICA *strides toward* MYSTERIOUS STRANGER *and removes his disguise, revealing a bald-headed man in his 40's.*

VERONICA: Allow me to introduce to you all, Archie Gathasit, Erich Thaaargist, Lady Hattie Chrisaga, Detective Peter Colhouri and, last but not least, my ex-husband, Gerald Edgeware!

WPC. HASTINGS: I don't understand.

VERONICA: Why are none of us surprised?

WALTER: And when were you going to tell me about this one, mother dear?!

MYSTERIOUS STRANGER: Oh, there's such a lot you don't know, young man.

LULU: So, you're neither an American <u>nor</u> a detective?

MYSTERIOUS STRANGER: Sorry, kid.

LULU: (*shrugs getting over it fast*) Oh well.

WALTER: (*holding out his hand to her*) You've still got me. (LULU *takes his hand and smiles affectionately*)

JEAN: (*returning with plates and napkins which she places on the table*) Well, one thing I know is that I'm famished.

SCRATCHY: How can you think of eating at a time like this, Jean?

JEAN: I've taken the liberty of baking something and would love you all to join me. Now, tea and treats that's the ticket. All these little problems will sort themselves out. They usually do. Lulu, would you be a dear and pop next door? There are a few more nibbles on my kitchen table. Take Walter with you. I expect you'd like to be private for a while. *(meaningfully)* You have a few things to discuss.

LULU: *(unsure but smiling)* But – oh, alright then.

LULU *and* WALTER *exit through the French doors hand in hand*

JEAN: *(as they go)* Take your time. (*she returns to the kitchen area*)

SCRATCHY: So, you are the Mysterious Strangers. Well, I have to take my hat off to you, boy, you had us bumpkins taken in good and proper.

JEAN: Tarquin said he could always spot a fellow thespian.

MYSTERIOUS STRANGER: *(bowing)* I've always loved the stage. It was where Veronica and I met. She was the best and the worst thing that had ever happened to me.

SCRATCHY: That's women for you all over.

VERONICA: If you men had an ounce of backbone...

JEAN: (*returning with a tray of tarts and cakes*) Please, tuck in. I made them myself.

SCRATCHY: (*waves JEAN away*) I couldn't.

JEAN: They're not for you, Scratchy. You need to watch your waistline.

WPC. HASTINGS: (*greedily*) I'll have his then. (HASTINGS *takes several cakes and begins eating immediately*)

MYSTERIOUS STRANGER: Now you come to mention it I've worked up quite an appetite. These look lovely. You say you baked them yourself? Sponge cake and...

JEAN: (*holding out plate to* VERONICA) Tart.

VERONICA: (*unimpressed by the jibe but takes a tart anyway*) Quite the homemaker, Jean. Did you never marry?

JEAN: No, sadly, most men do not see eye to eye with me. Though there is one who I might...but it wasn't meant to be.

VERONICA *and* MYSTERIOUS STRANGER *begin to eat.* HASTINGS *begins coughing violently.*

SCRATCHY: Don't eat so fast, it'll be the death of you.

WPC. HASTINGS: I don't feel so good. (*loosens her tie*) I think I...

HASTINGS *collapses making agonizing tortured sounds.* SCRATCHY *bends over her to see if he can help.*

SCRATCHY: (*numb*) She's – she's dead.

JEAN: Well, of course she is. The rate she was shoving them down it was bound to work very quickly. I expected them take at least 5 minutes, but this sort of thing is never an exact science.

VERONICA *and the* MYSTERIOUS STRANGER *look at one another with a realization of impending death.* SCRATCHY *is open mouthed.*

MYSTERIOUS STRANGER: You mean they're.......

JEAN: Apricot and marzipan.

MYSTERIOUS STRANGER: Poisoned!

VERONICA: (*to* JEAN) You bitch. I had everything to live for...oh Gerald...

VERONICA *falls, caught by* MYSTERIOUS STRANGER *who simultaneously falls with her, they slump gracefully together and end up propping each other up and holding grimly to each other.*

MYSTERIOUS STRANGER: I can taste almonds, that would be the cyanide I suppose.

JEAN: Top marks that man. You'd have made a fine real detective.

VERONICA: I'm so sorry, Gerald, to have gotten you involved in all this.

MYSTERIOUS STRANGER: Not to worry old thing. Glad we can finally be together.

VERONICA *and the* MYSTERIOUS STRANGER *die with a theatrical flourish, each trying to outdo the other.*

SCRATCHY: What the bloody hell have you done Jean Palmer?! You've just murdered three people.

JEAN: Good lord no - six by my tally. (*pause*) This year.

SCRATCHY: (*aghast*) Are you saying...you killed my sister, the Colonel and Tarquin, but why Jean, why?

JEAN: Because I could. Oh, don't look at me that way, you dear sweet man. None of them matter. They were all such insignificant people.

SCRATCHY: How could you? How did you?

JEAN: Oh, I didn't do it alone. My little angel helped me.

SCRATCHY: You're mad! Stark staring bonkers!

JEAN: No Scratchy. My darling Jack, don't you see? We can be together now. We have everything. We have these houses. Lulu and Walter will have the Manor House. Well, they'll need it if they're to raise a family of their own. These two houses will do for us. We can knock them back into one property again. We have plenty of money. Why these pearls alone will fetch a King's ransom and I still have most of the other treasure.

SCRATCHY: Treasure?

JEAN: I found it years ago. Just before I persuaded you to divide the cellar and brick up the well. I'm so glad I asked you to put that cat flap in

	though. It has proved to be very useful.
SCRATCHY:	Cat flap?
JEAN:	And now we are rich, and we can go anywhere in the world. (*taking his hand*) Stay with me always, Scratchy. Let's spread our wings and fly!
SCRATCHY:	Let's not. (*with his free hand he stuffs cake after cake into his mouth, fending off* JEAN's *attempts to stop him by holding her at arm's length. He quickly coughs and collapses. His wooden leg twitches noisily on the floor before he dies*)
SOUND FX:	A CAR PULLS UP ON GRAVEL OS

LULU *and* WALTER *are seen crossing from L to R outside the French doors.* WALTER *is carrying a tray with a few bowls on it.*

LULU: (*off*)	Well, wouldn't you know it? More police...careful with that tray, Walter.
WALTER: (*off*)	You sound just like my mother, but I love you anyway.

JEAN: That's a pity, sounds like the games up. (JEAN *goes towards French doors, stops, seeing something on the stairs DR, picks it up. It is a white cat.*) There you are my angel. Come to Mummy. What a pity our little game will not be rewarded. (*she looks out of the closed French doors towards offstage UR stroking the cat in her arms*)

SOUND FX: *(over the following speech).* CAR DOOR OPENS AND CLOSES. FEET ON GRAVEL. MUFFLED VOICES.

JEAN: (*she turns the key in the French doors to lock them*) What fun we've had. And you need a good wash and brush-up. All that too-ing and fro-ing through that cat flap has done you no good at all. What a magnificent species you are. What supreme intelligence. And they say you can't be trained. No wonder the ancient Egyptians worshipped you. (*moves slowly DC, stepping over dead bodies where necessary*) It was really very easy for you wasn't it my angel? Tripping Mavis on the cellar steps and then the Colonel. Yes, we got lucky with him

	and his infernal shotgun. All done under cover of darkness. You picked that up as quick as a flash using your perfect night vision. And the marmite on the lamp wires so that you'd know just where to nibble them - inspired! And then you nudged me when I was putting the poison in the cakes to make sure that I administered just the right amount, such a clever cat! A shame about Scratchy but it's just you and me again - just you and me.
LIGHTING FX:	LULU *and* WALTER *are seen approaching the French doors and trying the doors as the* LIGHTS FADE *to* BLACKOUT *and* JEAN *exits DR into the cellar.*
SOUND FX:	A CAT PURRING LOUDLY
SOUND FX*:*	*The* RADIOGRAM *sparks into life with soft lights and a few hisses and crackles.*
RADIO ANNOUNCER:	Here is the news from the BBC and this is Alvar Lidell reading it. Jean Palmer, the North Devon woman accused of being a multiple murderess is to be sentenced at the

Old Bailey today. The bill to end capital punishment is also being heard today and the question uppermost in most people's minds is 'will the woman believed to be responsible for the Cat Flap murders face the executioner's rope'?

SOUND FX: A CAT WAILS LOUDLY

CURTAIN

THE END

The Cat Flap

Properties List: Act One

The page number indicates the page that the character enters.

PAGE	CHARACTER	PROPERTIES
16	SET	Wall clock set at 6:58, tray, 12 cat bowls and large pan of cat food on kitchen table, scrubbing brush and burnt pan by sink, first aid kit by sink, teacloth hanging over the back of a chair, dust on chair, towel and face flannel in dresser.
16	Mavis	Lit cigarette, large ladle.
16	Scratchy	Dust on face and hands, spectacles held together with sticking plaster, working boots.
20	Lulu	Lipstick
22	Colonel	12-bore shotgun, transfer deed in pink ribbon.
26	Jean	String of pearls

Properties List: Act One (continued)

PAGE	CHARACTER	PROPERTIES
30	Walter	Wicker cat basket, horn-rimmed glasses, handkerchief
30	Veronica	Cigarettes, lighter and cigarette holder
40	Jean	Covered in dust (from cellar)
41	Jean	Long coil of rope (French doors)
42	Mavis	Bucket of water
46	Stranger	Floppy felt hat, white wig, cape, silver-topped cane.

Properties List: Act Two

PAGE	CHARACTER	PROPERTIES
61	SET	Wall clock set at 7:30, scrawny Christmas tree with fairy, home-made paper chain, two-bar electric fire, kettle on stove, tray, 8 cups and saucers, milk and sugar in kitchen, business card in letter-rack, biscuit barrel on dresser.
61	Jean	Paper and pen, string of pearls
62	Scratchy	Arm plaster
62	Hastings	Notebook and pencil
71	Veronica	Umbrella
71	Tarquin	Tape measure
89	Stranger	Snow on clothes, knife
95	Colonel	12-bore shotgun.

Properties List: Act Three, Scene One

PAGE	CHARACTER	PROPERTIES
101	SET	REMOVE: cattery pen, old outside light, gingham curtains, old dresser, kitchen table and chairs, old telephone. SET: new wall coverings, new backdrop, potted plant, new outside light, new kitchen units, ornamental cats on shelf, new telephone, new table and two new chairs, vase of flowers, bowl of fruit and lamp on table, drinking glass in kitchen. Wall clock set to 2:55.
102	Scratchy	New glasses, trilby hat
103	Jean	String of pearls, bunch of car keys, ornamental white cat
105	Walter	Tennis gear, spotted neckerchief, white headband, tennis racquet
108	Lulu	Bunch of flowers, 45rpm record in envelope.
110	Veronica	Floppy hat
111	Tarquin/ Hastings	Pampered Pussies sign.

Properties List: Act Three, Scene One (continued)

120	Stranger	Broad-brimmed feathered hat, lorgnette, high-heels, wicker basket, silver-topped cane
122	Scratchy	Wooden stepladder
136	Jean	Glass of brandy, magazine

Properties List: Act Three, Scene Two

PAGE	CHARACTER	PROPERTIES
139	SET	Wall clock set to 10:30, tray of clean cups and plates, plate of cakes, plate of tarts, small plates and napkins.
139	Jean	Cups
139	Hastings	Notebook and pencil
139	Scratchy	Head bandage
139	Jean	String of pearls, sheaf of notes
139	Veronica	Handkerchief, cigarettes, cigarette holder and lighter,
141	Stranger	Unlit cigarette, trilby hat, police badge, revolver
172	Lulu/Walter	Trays with bowls on
173	Jean	White cat

END OF PROPERTIES LISTS

Sound Effects: Act One

PAGE	CUE	EFFECT
16	Before curtain up	Hammering from cellar.
16	Before curtain up	Background noises of cats.
16	As curtain rises	'Give Seven' by The Bill McGuffie Quartet on radiogram.
16	Mavis first passes the telephone table	Telephone rings.
16	Mavis: …you ungrateful beasts!	Cats wail
16	Mavis: Wait your turn the rest of you.	Clatter of bowls thrown down followed by loud tapping noises from cellar.
17	Mavis enters through French doors.	Telephone rings.
17	Mavis exits French doors second time	Telephone rings followed by outside light buzzing as it goes out.

Sound Effects: Act One (continued)

PAGE	CUE	EFFECT
17	Scratchy enters DR	Radiogram announcement: News has just come in....
18	Mavis enters through French doors and turns off radiogram	Radiogram off
19	Scratchy exits through French doors	Motorbike pulling up followed by upstairs door opening and sounds of 'Please, Please Me' from bedroom.
20	Lulu walks back upstairs.	'Please, Please Me' stops.
20	Scratchy opens cat pen	Loud howling and wailing of cats.
21	Mavis: And what thanks do I get?	Motorbike horn.
22	Mavis: Just get it sorted......	Motorbike drives off.
22	Colonel: Damned infernal motorbikes!	Loud cat wails

Sound Effects: Act One (continued)

PAGE	CUE	EFFECT
23	Colonel: …if it's the last thing I do.	Cat wails
26	Colonel: Now put that brush down!	Chink, chink sounds from cellar (continues)
29	Mavis & Colonel: Shut up, Jean!	More tapping noises from cellar
36	Colonel: I'll say. (wait for twitches)	Loud crash and then a splash from cellar
38	WPC Hastings: Get out of the way!	Cat Wails
43	Colonel: Too much damned noise! (wait for plaster to fall)	Cats wail.
43	Mavis: …It'll take all night to settle them.	Loud crash and another splash from cellar
46	Tarquin: …This must be such an ordeal for you.	Doorbell rings

Sound Effects: Act One (continued)

PAGE	CUE	EFFECT
54	Veronica: That would be difficult. (wait until she leans on door frame)	Outside Light buzzes and flickers together
57	Walter: …. Mumsie, I'm just feeling a little…	Loud crash from cellar
60	Mavis screams in the blackout	Cat wails followed by radiogram fading in …. from our Washington correspondent etc.

Sound Effects: Act Two

PAGE	CUE	EFFECT
61	As the curtain rises,	I Want to Hold Your Hand by The Beatles on radiogram, leading into Radio DJs announcement and introduction to Blowin' in the Wind.
61	Mavis turns off radiogram.	Radiogram off
61	Jean opens French doors.	Wind howling.
72	Lulu opens French doors.	Wind howling.
85	Jean opens French doors.	Wind howling.
87	Walter: What happened to him?	Doorbell rings followed by the 'fizzing' of lights in the subsequent blackout.
87	Veronica: I don't know, I'm not psychic. (pause)	Doorbell rings followed by sound of lights 'spluttering'.

Sound Effects: Act Two (continued)

PAGE	CUE	EFFECT
88	Hastings: I Suppose I should go. (pause)	Doorbell rings long and loud
98	Jean opens French doors.	Wind howling followed by the sound of the outside light spluttering on
99	Colonel: Watch out! He's got a weapon! (lights flicker)	'Buzzing' s outside light flicker followed by wind howling.
99	Walter et al: Where's the candles? etc...	A cat screeches.
100	Colonel's gun goes off.	Outside light 'buzzes' as it flickers followed by wind howling
100	Lulu screams	Radiogram on – In the Bleak Mid-Winter

Sound Effects: <u>Act Three, Scene One</u>

PAGE	CUE	EFFECT
101	Just before the curtain rises	Radiogram plays Zambezi by Lou Busch. Sounds of birdsong in the background
102	Scratchy changes the programme on the radiogram	Radiogram crackles and changes to Gardening Programme (So, Percy, it's that time of year...)
103	Lulu changes the programme on the radiogram	Radiogram changes to I Want to Hold Your Hand by The Beatles
103	Jean changes the programme on the radiogram	Radiogram crackles and whistles and fades into tennis commentary (Tennis balls being hit, Oh, I say, that's a magnificent return...)
105	Lulu turns off radiogram.	Radiogram stops. Birdsong continues occasionally until Veronica's entrance.

Sound Effects: Act Three, Scene One (continued)

PAGE	CUE	EFFECT
109	Veronica: (*off*) …It can't be that heavy.	Birdsong stops.
116	Veronica: …People will be able to see it from the road…	Hard Day's Night by The Beatles heard faintly from upstairs bedroom.
118	Tarquin: Outside with it again then!	Music stops
120	Veronica: …how dare you, you frustrated old hag!	Doorbell rings
120	Veronica: …just signed your death warrant, Jean Palmer.	Doorbell rings
131	Veronica: Tarquin!	A Hard Day's Night by The Beatles heard from upstairs bedroom. Music continues on a loop.
137	Tarquin: …I hate Marmite. (turns on lamp)	Bulb explodes, music stops, sound of high electrical current.

Sound Effects: Act Three, Scene Two (continued)

PAGE	CUE	EFFECT
172	Scratchy: Let's not. (*dies, wait for wooden leg to stop twitching*)	A car pulls up on gravel outside.
173	Jean: …What a pity our little game will not be rewarded.	Car door opening and closing, muffled voices, feet on gravel.
174	Jean: …just you and me again – just you and me.	Cat purring loudly followed immediately by radiogram coming to life: "Here is the news from the BBC", followed immediately by a cat wailing loudly.
175	Curtain, House lights up	Incidental Music – Zambezi by Lou Busch

END OS SOUND EFFECTS

Lighting Effects: Act One

PAGE	CUE	EFFECT
16	Start of Act One	An autumn evening. Kitchen lit by electric lights. Outside is gloomy.
16	Mavis turns on OS light.	Mavis turns on OS light.
17	Jean slams phone down.	OS light buzzes and goes off.
31	Veronica stands under OS light framed by the French doors.	OS light flickers and comes on.
32	Veronica steps inside	OS goes off.
54	Veronica leans against door frame	OS light flickers and comes on and mirror light comes on at same time.
57	Veronica: ...little chocolate soldier. I'm here! (wait for her to move away from French doors)	OS light and mirror light go off.

Lighting Effects: Act One (continued)

PAGE	CUE	EFFECT
60	Mavis: ...You still down there?	All lights flicker and buzz.
60	Mavis steps inside through the cellar door	All lights flicker then blackout.
60	After scream and cat wail	OS light flickers and we see lights in the radiogram as it sparks into life.
60	*Radiogram* Leonard Parkin: ...President Kennedy is dead. (curtain)	House lights up

Lighting Effects: Act Two

PAGE	CUE	EFFECT
61	Start of Act Two	Winter evening/ Kitchen lit by electric lights. Outside is dark.
62	Jean turns off radiogram.	Bright lights of a vehicle's headlights OS
72	Lulu opens the French doors with Veronica standing in doorway.	OS light flickers and comes on.
73	Veronica: Well, I simply must get warm. (moves away from French doors)	OS light goes off.
87	Walter: …What happened to him? (Doorbell rings)	As the bell rings the lights flicker and blackout
87	Walter screams	Lights come back on
87	Veronica: …I'm not psychic. (pause, doorbell rings)	Lights flicker.

Lighting Effects: Act Two (continued)

PAGE	CUE	EFFECT
98	Jean wrenches open French doors.	OS light flickers and comes on. All the lights flicker, and the radiogram throws out static.
99	Colonel: Watch out! He's got a weapon! (Hastings is knocked to the floor)	All the lights, including the OS light, flicker but stay on
99	Jean: What's going on?	Blackout
100	Colonel's gun goes off.	Outside light flickers and comes on briefly followed by a blackout. Kitchen lights come up after 5 seconds.
100	Curtain falls	Fade up house lights slowly during 'In the Bleak Mid-Winter'.

Lighting Effects: Act Three, Scene One

PAGE	CUE	EFFECT
101	Start of Act Three, Scene One	Mid-afternoon on a bright and sunny summer's day.
137	Veronica screams	Blackout. House lights stay off during scene change.

Act Three, Scene Two

PAGE	CUE	EFFECT
139	Start of Act Three, Scene Two – Veronica screams.	Quickly fade in lights - late-afternoon on a bright and sunny summer's day.
174	Lulu and Walter approach the French doors and try the handles, Jean starts to exit D.	Slow fade to blackout
175	Curtain	House lights on

END OF LIGHTING EFFECTS

Visual Effects: Act One

PAGE	CUE	EFFECT
43	Colonel: Too much damned noise!	Light shower of plaster from kitchen ceiling
43	Loud crash and splash from cellar	Cloud of dust through cellar door

Visual Effects: Act Two

PAGE	CUE	EFFECT
71	Hastings: I think I might need to talk to the Colonel.	Snow starts to fall OS.
71	Excited voices off	Snow falls more heavily.
85	Jean: Yes, I know it's Christmas Eve. Snowing?	Blizzard outside
98	Jean: But Colonel, look outside. It's a blizzard now... (Jean wrenches open French doors)	Violent blizzard which blows inside when the French doors are opened.

END OF VISUAL EFFECTS

Printed in Great Britain
by Amazon